# The Daily Bean

··· a cookbook ···

# The Daily Bean

· · · · · · · · · · · · · · · · ·

175 Easy and Creative Bean Recipes
for Breakfast, Lunch, Dinner,
and...yes, Dessert!

· · · · · · · · · · · · · · · · ·

## Suzanne Caciola White

LifeLine
Press®

A Regnery Publishing Company, Washington, D.C.

Library of Congress Cataloging-in-Publication Data on file.

ISBN 0-89526-071-9

Published in the United States by
LifeLine Press
A Regnery Publishing Company
One Massachusetts Avenue, N.W.
Washington, DC 20001

Visit us at www.lifelinepress.com

Distributed to the trade by
National Book Network
4720-A Boston Way
Lanham, MD 20706

Printed on acid-free paper

Manufactured in the United States of America

10  9  8  7  6  5  4  3  2  1

Books are available in quantity for promotional or premium use. Write to Director of Special Sales, Regnery Publishing, Inc., One Massachusetts Avenue, N.W., Washington, DC 20001, for information on discounts and terms or call (202) 216-0600.

The information contained in this book is not a substitute for medical counseling and care. All matters pertaining to your physical health should be supervised by a health care professional.

# Contents

# Preface

Several years ago, my husband was diagnosed with diabetes. His desire to explore both traditional and alternative treatment options led him to a naturopath doctor, who recommended that he discontinue his consumption of red meat and bring beans into his diet three times a day. Barely able to contain his enthusiasm, my husband requested that I shoot him.

Despite his initial qualms, my husband and I soon learned that the doctor's orders were more than just doable—they were delicious! After countless hours in the kitchen experimenting with exciting combinations of beans, herbs, spices, fruits, and vegetables, I have developed a bean repertoire to impress even the most epicurean palate. These recipes I've created, and those that have come to me through friends, family, and fellow chefs, I am now delighted to share with you in this rare and wonderful collection.

Have fun with these recipes—we certainly did. Happy cooking!

# Introduction

*Beans, beans — beautiful beans!* Our knowledge of beans is immense. We've consumed them for thousands of years, and they are a staple in almost every known cuisine. Whether revered by the masses and reserved for kings or used to save entire populations from starvation, beans have left their mark on our world.

We can even find references to the bean's healing and nourishing properties in the Bible. Citations in the books of Samuel and Ezekiel indicate that the hearty bean was believed to heal the sick and injured.

Today, we are rediscovering what people of old knew so well—that the bean has much more to offer than taste alone. Beans, and legumes in general, are a rich source of protein, calcium, phosphorus, fiber, and iron.

Their high protein content, combined with the fact that they're so easily grown and stored, especially the dried varieties, make beans a staple throughout the world, particularly where animal protein might be scarce. In this era, when many Americans are trying to cut down on red meat, beans serve as a high-flavor, low-cost substitute.

The protein found in beans is nearly as high in quality as that in meat, eggs, or dairy products. You can easily—and deliciously—make up for the missing amino acids by serving your beans with brown rice (or any grain), nuts, or cheese. By doing so, you are actually producing the perfect protein. Your muscle cells will never know that the amino acids came from plants instead of animals.

While protein is a plus for anyone, the fact that beans are fat free with approximately 100 calories per half-cup serving is an added bonus for dieters. Beans also digest slowly and cause a low, sustained increase in blood sugar, thereby acting as a natural appetite suppressant and enhancing most weight-loss programs safely and nutritiously.

The bean's extremely high fiber content is perfect for people needing to lower their cholesterol levels. In a recent study, a group of men added beans to their diet, and their cholesterol levels dropped sixty points in just three weeks. And a half a cup a day will do it. Also, despite the high carbohydrate content, the soluble fiber found in beans leads to a low glycemic index. The glycemic index is a measure of a food's effect on blood sugar levels, and it depends on how rapidly its carbohydrates are absorbed. Bread, potatoes, cereals, and rice have a high glycemic index similar to table sugar, but beans have a low glycemic index—making them a great food for diabetics.

The fiber content of beans also makes them a great weapon against various gastrointestinal woes. If used as an integral part of your diet, beans can help prevent and cure constipation. Regular consumption of this wonder-food can also stop hemorrhoids and other bowel-related problems from developing or help cure them if they already exist.

In addition to providing a wide variety of B-complex vitamins, especially folic acid and B6 (which are lacking in the average American diet), beans are also a good source of magnesium, zinc, and copper—minerals essential to a healthy immune system. Magnesium is helpful in hypertension, heart disorders, insomnia, fatigue, anxiety, and menopause, and copper is also beneficial to arthritis, various heart disorders, and anemia.

As if the bean wasn't already a near-perfect food, many researchers are now saying that beans can help prevent cancer. Beans contain high amounts of slightly mysterious, estrogen-blocking substances called phytoestrogens, which are reported to protect against colon cancer. They also contain protease inhibitors, which have been found to reverse the initial cancer-causing damage to cells in studies conducted on tissue cultures. Some researchers also believe that protease inhibitors may prove useful in combating viruses as well as many forms of cancer.

On top of what beans in general have to offer, specific kinds of beans often have unique beneficial properties of their own. Winged beans, for example, contain erucic acid, which is extracted to formulate an antitumor medication. And soybeans produce the same omega-3 oils (linoleic acid) found in fish, which shore the cardiovascular system against disease.

If you can think of a reason not to welcome beans into your life, I'd like to hear it. I invite you to use this handbook to incorporate this wonderful ingredient into your life. You'll find so much more here than Boston Baked Beans and Mom's succotash, and you'll learn how to create the extraordinary from the ordinary while enjoying greater health.

The recipes in this book range from basic, traditional fare to gourmet dishes that will delight even the epicurean palate. Imaginative combinations of herbs, spices, fruits, and vegetables will help you incorporate this wonder food into your diet with gusto. Once you savor these dishes, you'll become a true believer as you witness the improvements in your health. Or you may just enjoy good, wholesome food.

# Beans Done Right

This list of simple dos and don'ts will guide your venture into this new realm of cooking (and help you adjust your system to the infamous side effects of consuming legumes):

. . . . . . . . . . . . .

Introduce beans often, but in small amounts at the beginning. This will help establish a beneficial bacteria that will deal with the complex sugars (oligosaccharides) that produce gas in the bowels. In time, you will be able to eat larger amounts with no discomfort.

. . . . . . . . . . . . .

Start with lentils, black-eyed peas, white beans, chickpeas, and lima beans. They may not produce as much gas.

. . . . . . . . . . . . .

Do not cook beans in the soaking water; the complex sugars would be re-absorbed. Instead, rinse the beans and add fresh water. You may lose some of the water-soluble nutrients, but more than adequate food value will remain.

. . . . . . . . . . . . .

Always drain the liquid from canned legumes and rinse them thoroughly in a strainer. You are not only discarding the sugars but also about 40 percent of the sodium added during processing.

. . . . . . . . . . . . .

. . . .

. . . . . . . . . . . . . .

Never add salt to the soaking water. It will toughen the seed coat and prevent water absorption. Only add salt to the cooking beans after they are tender; otherwise, the skin will become impermeable and the liquids will not be absorbed.

. . . . . . . . . . . . .

Always simmer beans slowly; don't boil.

. . . . . . . . . . . . .

Never add acidic ingredients (e.g., tomato, lemon, or pineapple) before the beans are tender. They will never soften after you add the acidic ingredient.

. . . . . . . . . . . . .

The liquid preparation Beano will start digesting the offending sugars immediately. Only a few drops on the first bite will do the trick.

. . . . . . . . . . . . .

To get the full nutritional benefit of legumes, again, gradually increase the amount until you are consuming at least three to four cups of beans, peas, or lentils per week.

. . . . . . . . . . . . .

. . . . .

# Recipe Hints

**BLACK BEAN SAUCE** can be found in the Asian foods section of your grocery store.

**BRAGGS AMINO ACIDS** is a soy sauce substitute—lower in sodium, comparable in taste. It can be found in any health food store.

**CHILI PASTE** pops up a few times in these recipes. You can find it in an Asian market or sometimes in the Asian foods section of a good grocery store.

**COCONUT MILK** can be found in the Indian or gourmet section of your grocery store. There is no sugar in coconut milk, so don't confuse it with the cream of coconut mix used to make piña coladas.

**HOT SAUCE** is a must, and my bottle of choice is usually Tabasco or Texas Pete. But any sauce should do the trick. Just make sure you know what you're getting yourself into!

**MEAT** can be added easily and elegantly to most of the recipes here (except the desserts, of course!). On those occasions when you're looking for an extra protein kick, or have some savory leftovers to use up, toss in some shredded chicken, slices of sweet or spicy sausage, some cubed ham, or even bacon. Here are some suggestions:

Shredded chicken in Lemon Lentil Soup
Chicken thighs in Moroccan Lentil Soup
Sweet sausage in Lentil Stew
Cubed ham steaks in Red Bean Soup
Chicken in Florentine Beans and Pasta
Sweet sausage in Linguini with Chickpeas and Anchovies
Real bacon in Garbanzos Fritos
Chorizo sausage in Cuban Black Bean Soup

**MISO** is a fermented bean paste that can be found in an Asian market or health food store. It comes in several varieties, including white, red, and dark.

**MOJO, RECAITO, AND SAZÓN** are seasonings or marinades found in the Spanish or Mexican section of any good grocery store. Sazón comes in a box of packets. Criollo, Achote y Cilantro, and Anato are a few of the flavor options.

**SPLENDA AND STEVIA** are excellent nonnutritive sugar substitutes. Splenda can be found in most major grocery stores and is used cup-for-cup as a sugar substitute. Stevia, a potent herbal sweetener found in any health food store, is a healthful consideration for anyone who must avoid refined sugars. It comes in both powdered and liquid form.

**VEGETABLE BROTH** can be substituted for chicken broth in any recipe. The tasteful beans and spices will more than make up for any flavor differences.

# Standard Bean Soaking and Cooking Table

Canned beans are just precooked dried beans and are completely interchangeable in any recipe. Most recipes will call for canned beans for convenience' sake only.

The following is a chart for the cold-water method of soaking and cooking dried legumes. Soaking is the first step in using dried beans, and it serves two functions. First, it rehydrates the bean, and second, it removes some of the indigestible sugars that create gas in some people. The standard soaking method calls for 10 cups of water for every pound of beans. For the longer soaking times, change the soaking water at least once. After soaking, drain and rinse the beans thoroughly. Cover the soaked beans with fresh water and simmer over low heat until the beans are tender.

Bean dishes freeze wonderfully, so any extra time in soaking or cooking can be put into a dish that will be frozen to save time on another day.

| | Soaking Time* | Cooking Time** |
|---|---|---|
| Adzuki | 4 hours | 1 hour |
| Black beans | 4 hours | 1–1½ hours |
| Lima beans | 4 hours | 1–1½ hours |
| Cannellini beans | 4 hours | 1–1½ hours |
| Garbanzo beans (chickpeas) | 4 hours | 2½ hours |
| Fava beans (broad beans) | 12 hours | 3 hours |
| Great northern beans | 4 hours | 1½–2 hours |
| Mung beans | 4 hours | 45 minutes–1 hour |
| Whole peas | 4 hours | 40 minutes |
| Pink, calico, or Red Mexican beans | 4 hours | 1½–2 hours |
| Pinto beans | 4 hours | 2–2½ hours |
| Red pinto beans | 4 hours | 1–1½ hours |
| White kidney beans | 4 hours | 1 hour |
| Small white (navy) beans | 4 hours | 1½–2 hours |
| Soybeans | 12 hours | 3–4 hours |

The following beans do not need soaking and can be cooked immediately.

| | Cooking Time |
|---|---|
| Black-eyed peas | 1–1¼ hours |
| Dals | 30 minutes |
| Brown lentils | 30–40 minutes |
| Green lentils | 40–50 minutes |
| Red lentils | 30–45 minutes |
| Split peas | 45 minutes–1 hour |
| Pigeon peas | 30 minutes |

* If you're pressed for time, you can cut the soaking time in half by boiling the beans for 2 to 3 minutes before beginning the soaking process.

** The average yield is 2¼ to 2½ cups cooked beans for every dry cup used.

# The Daily Bean: A Nutritional Guide

Nutritional values for 1 cup of cooked beans

| | | White Beans | | | |
|---|---|---|---|---|---|
| | Black Beans | Great Northern | Cannellini | Navy | Garbanzo |
| Calories | 227 | 209 | 225 | 258 | 286 |
| Protein (g) | 15 | 15 | 15 | 16 | 12 |
| Carbohydrates (g) | 41 | 37 | 40 | 48 | 54 |
| Total fat (g) | 1 | 1 | 1 | 1 | 3 |
| Fiber (g) | 15 | 12 | 11 | 12 | 11 |
| Calcium (mg) | 48 | 120 | 69 | 128 | 80 |
| Iron (mg) | 4 | 4 | 5 | 5 | 4 |
| Magnesium (mg) | 120 | 89 | 80 | 106 | 70 |
| Phosphorus (mg) | 241 | 356 | trace | 351 | 216 |
| Folate (mcg) | 256 | 181 | 229 | 255 | 160 |
| Vitamin B6 (mg) | trace | trace | 1 | trace | 1 |
| Vitamin C (mg) | trace | 3 | trace | 2 | 9 |
| Zinc (mg) | 2 | 2 | 7 | 2 | 3 |
| Selenium (mcg) | 6 | 26 | 3 | 22 | 6 |
| Potassium (mg) | 632 | 920 | 993 | 790 | 413 |
| Niacin (mg) | 1 | 1 | 1 | 1 | trace |

| | | Red Beans | | | |
|---|---|---|---|---|---|
| | Kidney | Small Red | Pinto | Adzuki | Lentils |
| Calories | 225 | 226 | 234 | 294 | 229 |
| Protein (g) | 15 | 16 | 14 | 17 | 18 |
| Carbohydrates (g) | 40 | 40 | 44 | 57 | 40 |
| Total fat (g) | 1 | trace | 1 | trace | 1 |
| Fiber (g) | 11 | 8 | 15 | 17 | 16 |
| Calcium (mg) | 78 | 50 | 82 | 86 | 38 |
| Iron (mg) | 5 | 6 | 5 | 5 | 7 |
| Magnesium (mg) | 80 | 80 | 65 | 120 | 71 |
| Phosphorus (mg) | 814 | 814 | 221 | 386 | 356 |
| Folate (mcg) | 229 | 230 | 294 | 278 | 357 |
| Vitamin B6 (mg) | trace | trace | trace | trace | trace |
| Vitamin C (mg) | 9 | 9 | 9 | trace | 3 |
| Zinc (mg) | 3 | 3 | 2 | 4 | 3 |
| Selenium (mcg) | 6 | 6 | 12 | 6 | 16 |
| Potassium (mg) | 629 | 629 | 583 | 1,223 | 730 |
| Niacin (mg) | 2 | 2 | 1 | 2 | 2 |

# Black Beans

# Black Beans

## a.k.a. Turtle Beans

*B*lack beans, also known as turtle beans, are a member of the kidney bean family. These small, dark, brownish-black beans are best known for their starring role in Cuban black bean soup, though they are commonly used throughout Central and South America and even China. Beneath their dark shell is a white meat with a hearty flavor, and, when cooked, they give a dark tint to any other ingredients cooked with them.

Their hearty flavor makes black beans hold up well to strong spices and seasonings. Don't be shy with the chili powder, cilantro, thyme, oregano, cumin, or any other bold Mexican, Southwestern, or Mediterranean spices these recipes may call for. And if you're experimenting on your own, remember that the black bean's extraordinary love affair with garlic and onions can almost always be enhanced by lemon juice or olive oil.

### Nutritional values for 1 cup of cooked black beans

Calories 227   Protein 15.2 g   Carbohydrates 40.8 g   Total fat 0.9 g   Fiber 15 g
Calcium 48 mg   Iron 3.61 mg   Magnesium 120 mg   Phosphorus 241 mg   Folate 256 mcg

## APPETIZERS

*Black Bean Dip*

*Black Salsa*

*Mango Black Bean Salsa*

*Baguette Toasts with Black Bean "Caviar"*

*Quesadillas with Black Beans and Cheese*

*Shrimp and Black Bean Lumpias*

*Black Bean Bruschetta*

## SALADS, SOUPS & SIDES

*Greek Bean Salad*

*Spicy Black Bean Salad*

*Black Bean, Barley, and Pine Nut Salad*

*Crab and Black Bean Bisque*

*Cuban Black Bean Soup*

*Black Bean Minestrone*

*José Jesus Iglasias's Mimma's Cuban Black Beans*

*Black Bean Corn Fritters*

## MAIN DISHES

*Margie Montalvo's Puerto Rican Black Beans*

*Spicy Black Bean Pizza*

*Black Bean Curry*

*Black-Hearted Chili*

*Black Bean Chili with Sherry*

*Huevos Rancheros with Black Beans*

*Spirals with Black Bean Salsa and Grape Tomatoes*

*Black Bean Burritos*

*Black Bean Pancakes*

*Brazilian Black Beans*

## DESSERTS

*Black Bean Almondine Flan*

*Heavenly Chocolate Almond Raspberry Black Bean Torte*

*Double Chocolate Walnut Black Bean Bread*

*Big, Bad Black Bean Brownies*

*Chocolate Walnut Bean Truffles*

*Chocolate Almond Black Bean Cheesecake*

*Fake' Em Out Fudge*

# Appetizers

## BLACK BEAN DIP

6 SERVINGS

An all-time favorite. Very easily prepared and a wonderful appetizer before any meal.

---

2 15.5-ounce cans black beans, drained and rinsed

½ cup chicken broth (or vegetable broth)

2 cloves garlic, minced

4 tablespoons fresh lime juice

2 teaspoons ground cumin

1 jalapeño pepper, seeded and finely chopped

pinch of salt, to taste

2 tablespoons chopped fresh cilantro, plus extra for garnish

1 large tomato, finely chopped

---

Combine the first seven ingredients in a food processor and blend until smooth. Fold in the chopped cilantro and tomatoes. Garnish with extra fresh cilantro. Cover with plastic wrap and chill for at least an hour to allow the flavors to blend.

Serve with large, restaurant-style corn chips and ice-cold margaritas and watch a sunset somewhere.

*Per serving:* calories 154, calories from fat 7, total fat 1 g, cholesterol 0 mg, carbohydrates 28 g, fiber 10 g, protein 10 g

# BLACK SALSA

4 TO 6 SERVINGS

One of the best things about black beans is that any other vegetables you use with them stand out like stars in a midnight sky. This recipe is a great example of this striking effect.

---

1 15.5-ounce can black beans, drained and rinsed

3 plum tomatoes, diced

2 tablespoons chopped jalapeño

¼ cup diced red onion

¼ cup chopped scallions (both white and green parts)

½ cup diced sweet red pepper

2 tablespoons white vinegar

1 tablespoon vegetable oil

---

Mix all ingredients well; cover and chill for at least 1 hour.

This variation of salsa has a bit more kick with the addition of the jalapeño pepper.

You can serve this over a salad, with chips, or as an excellent side salsa with chicken or fish.

*Per serving:* calories 170, calories from fat 4, total fat 4 g, cholesterol 0 mg, carbohydrates 27 g, fiber 9 g, protein 8 g

# MANGO BLACK BEAN SALSA

ABOUT 8 SERVINGS

Having spent quite a bit of time in Puerto Rico, I know that the mango season can be overwhelming. Even though I love mangos, I actually remember telling a dear friend, Nelson Montalvo, "Please, no more mangos!" as he waited for me at his fence with his daily gift of a whole bagful. This recipe, just one of many uses for the fruit, was developed out of desperation to use them up.

---

1 15.5-ounce can black beans, drained and rinsed

1 7-ounce can whole kernel corn, drained

½ red pepper, diced

1 medium-size mango, peeled and cut into small cubes

¼ cup diced red onion

¼ cup chopped fresh cilantro

2 tablespoons fresh lime juice

¼ teaspoon ground cumin

a good sprinkle of garlic powder (about ½ teaspoon)

---

Combine all ingredients and stir gently. Let sit for at least 1 hour to let the flavors blend. Warm white-corn tortilla chips do justice to this flavorful alternative to a plain old bean dip.

If you are feeling particularly creative, this salsa looks stunning when served in a hollowed-out pineapple half. Use the chunks of pineapple that you cut out to garnish the serving platter, but only if you are out to impress.

Great with mango daiquiris.

*Per serving:* calories 126, calories from fat 4, total fat 1 g, cholesterol 0 mg, carbohydrates 24 g, fiber 8 g, protein 7 g

# BAGUETTE TOASTS WITH BLACK BEAN "CAVIAR"

6 SERVINGS

This great appetizer can be served on either a silver platter or a plastic plate. The garnish will decide which.

## "Caviar"

1 15.5-ounce can black beans, drained and rinsed

2 tablespoons minced garlic

½ medium onion, chopped

1 teaspoon lemon juice

2 tablespoons olive oil

kosher salt to taste

Place above ingredients into a food processor and purée slightly until coarsely chopped but not smooth.

## Toppings

3 hardboiled eggs, chopped

sour cream

3 scallions, chopped (both white and green parts)

## Baguette

1 baguette loaf, sliced into slices ¼ inch thick

olive oil spray

fresh ground black pepper

Preheat oven to 450° F.

Spray baguette slices on both sides with the olive oil spray.

Sprinkle fresh ground pepper on one side. Arrange in a single layer on a cookie sheet and toast in oven until golden on one side; turn and "golden" the other sides. While still warm, top with the black bean "caviar," putting approximately 2 tablespoons of the bean mixture on each toast. Then top with the chopped eggs, sour cream, and chopped scallions.

If you place the toasts on a silver platter, garnished with fresh parsley and tiny grape tomatoes, you'll be a star!

*Per serving for "caviar" and topping:* calories 98, calories from fat 42, total fat 5 g, cholesterol 72 mg, carbohydrates 9 g, fiber 3 g, protein 5 g

# QUESADILLAS WITH BLACK BEANS AND CHEESE

8 SERVINGS

This is a perfect summertime appetizer, easy to put together and easy to make more of, as you will most surely need to do.

---

1 15.5-ounce can black beans, drained and rinsed

1 large tomato, diced

1 jalapeño pepper, diced

1 roasted sweet red pepper, finely chopped

1 tablespoon minced garlic

½ cup fresh cilantro, finely chopped

3 tablespoons scallions, chopped (both white and green parts)

1 cup cheddar cheese, shredded

1 cup Monterey jack cheese, shredded

6 large (10-inch) flour tortillas

Preheat oven to 375° F.

Combine black beans, tomato, peppers, garlic, cilantro, and scallions.

Spoon mixture over half of each tortilla, sprinkle with cheeses, and fold over.

Place on a large cookie sheet that has been sprayed with oil and heat in oven for 8 to 10 minutes, or until cheese has melted and almost bubbled. (These can also be done on an outside grill. Brush the grill with olive oil and grill quesadillas for 2 to 3 minutes per side.)

Cut each tortilla into 3 wedges and serve on a warm platter, garnished with fresh cilantro sprigs.

Find a patio and serve with a pitcher of Sangria.

*Per serving:* calories 302, calories from fat 115, total fat 13 g, cholesterol 32 mg, carbohydrates 31 g, fiber 4 g, protein 16 g

# SHRIMP AND BLACK BEAN LUMPIAS

15 SERVINGS

This eggroll-like appetizer, with its crunchy exterior and flavorful filling, will do a disappearing act at any gathering.

2 cups dried black beans

1 tablespoon plus 1 teaspoon chili powder (divided use)

2 tablespoons olive oil

½ cup diced red onions

½ cup diced red peppers

1 teaspoon ground cumin

kosher salt and black pepper to taste

¼ cup chicken broth (or vegetable broth)

2 cups small raw shrimp

2 tablespoons chopped cilantro

1 package spring roll wrappers, 30–35 rolls

oil for deep frying

Soak black beans in water to cover; drain, replace water, and cook black beans with 1 tablespoon of the chili powder. Add salt the last 30 minutes of cooking. Let cool and drain beans.

In a large sauté pan, heat oil and sauté onions and peppers with cumin, the remaining teaspoon of chili powder, salt, and pepper until vegetables are soft. Add the beans and broth. Cook until mixture is moist but not soupy. Add the shrimp the last 3 minutes of cooking.

Let mixture cool, stir in cilantro, and roll in the spring roll wrappers, tucking in the ends of the wrappers.

Fry in oil about 2 inches deep at 375° F until golden brown.

*Per serving (filling):* calories 48, calories from fat 3, total fat 0 g, cholesterol 22 mg, carbohydrates 7 g, fiber 2 g, protein 5 g (See original packaging for spring roll nutrition information.)

# BLACK BEAN BRUSCHETTA

8 SERVINGS

This typically Italian appetizer gets a Southwest kick in this recipe. Black beans easily lend themselves to this flavor.

---

1 loaf French bread, cut into 16 slices

olive oil spray with garlic

fresh ground black pepper

1 cup canned black beans, drained and rinsed

1 cup chopped tomato

¼ cup green pepper, chopped

2 tablespoons onion, finely chopped

1 tablespoon fresh cilantro, chopped

3 tablespoons olive oil

2 tablespoons fresh lime juice

pinch of kosher salt to taste

¼ teaspoon ground cumin

¼ teaspoon oregano

1 teaspoon crushed garlic

½ cup Monterey Jack cheese

½ cup cheddar cheese

---

Preheat oven to 400° F.

Spray the slices of French bread with the garlic olive oil spray on both sides. Lightly toast in oven until golden on one side, turn over, sprinkle with the fresh pepper and golden brown the other side. Watch these carefully—they don't take long and they burn easily.

Combine the next five ingredients. In a small bowl, whisk together the olive oil, lime juice, salt, cumin, oregano, and garlic. Toss with the bean mixture.

Divide the bean mixture evenly over the French bread toasts and sprinkle evenly with the cheeses. Broil 6 inches from the heat until cheese melts and bubbles, about 3 minutes.

Serve immediately.

*Per serving for topping:* calories 127, calories from fat 75, total fat 9 g, cholesterol 10 mg, carbohydrates 7 g, fiber 2 g, protein 6 g

# Salads, Soups & Sides

## GREEK BEAN SALAD

6 SERVINGS

This salad is high in protein and easy to prepare. Though you can make it throughout the year, it's at its most flavorful during the summer, when the vegetables are at their freshest.

2 15.5-ounce cans black beans, drained and rinsed

2 red bell peppers, diced

1 medium-size cucumber, peeled and cut into ½-inch cubes

½ cup chopped fresh parsley

12 large leaves red leaf lettuce

½ red onion, thinly sliced

⅔ cup crumbled feta cheese

fresh ground black pepper to taste

Combine beans, peppers, cucumber, and parsley in a mixing bowl.

### Dressing

3 tablespoons olive oil

2 tablespoons balsamic vinegar

¼ teaspoon garlic powder

½ teaspoon Splenda (or other nonnutritive sweetener)

1 teaspoon Dijon mustard

1 teaspoon lemon juice

small dash Worcestershire sauce

Whisk together all ingredients in a small bowl.

Add dressing to the bean mixture and toss well. Serve over the red curly lettuce and top with feta cheese, red onion, and fresh-ground black pepper.

Opa!

*Per serving:* calories 273, calories from fat 98, total fat 11 g, cholesterol 15 mg, carbohydrates 32 g, fiber 11 g, protein 13 g

# SPICY BLACK BEAN SALAD

4 TO 6 SERVINGS

This spicy and colorful salad makes an excellent side dish for a grilled fish dinner. It also makes an excellent lunch main course served over curly lettuce with ciabatta bread. A glass of cold, crisp Pinot Grigio rounds it out nicely.

---

- 2 15.5-ounce cans black beans, drained and rinsed
- 1 bunch of fresh cilantro, stemmed and chopped
- 8 grape or cherry tomatoes, halved, or 1 large tomato, chopped
- 1 yellow pepper, diced
- 2 tablespoons balsamic vinegar
- 1 tablespoon chili paste with garlic
- 1 tablespoon vegetable oil

---

Gently stir together all the ingredients and let sit for at least an hour. Serving this with a sliced mango on the side will not only add more color and look beautiful, but the sweetness of the mangos will cool and complement the spice of the chili paste.

*Per serving:* calories 176, calories from fat 27, total fat 3 g, cholesterol 0 mg, carbohydrates 29 g, fiber 10 g, protein 10 g

# BLACK BEAN, BARLEY, AND PINE NUT SALAD

6 TO 8 SERVINGS

The bean and barley combination makes this dish a perfect protein source—not to mention an absolutely delicious salad.

---

1 cup barley (not quick-cooking)

6 tablespoons lemon juice

1 tablespoon Dijon mustard

salt and pepper to taste

¾ cup olive oil

3 15.5-ounce cans black beans, drained and rinsed

1½ cups finely chopped red onion

1 pound raw green beans, trimmed and cut into ¼-inch pieces

½ cup pine nuts, lightly toasted

---

Combine barley with 4 cups boiling salted water and simmer, covered, for 45 minutes or until cooked but still *al dente*. Drain barley, rinse, and drain well again.

In a small bowl, combine lemon juice, mustard, salt, and pepper. Add oil in a thin stream, whisking as you add until dressing is emulsified (thickened).

In a larger bowl, combine the beans, barley, and onion. Pour dressing over the bean mixture and toss until well mixed.

In a saucepan of boiling water, cook the green beans for 4 to 5 minutes until crisp-tender; drain and rinse immediately under cold water.

Add the green beans and pine nuts to the black bean mixture and toss well once more.

Serve chilled or at room temperature.

*Per serving:* calories 397, calories from fat 204, total fat 23 g, cholesterol 0 mg, carbohydrates 37 g, fiber 12 g, protein 13 g

# CRAB AND BLACK BEAN BISQUE

6 SERVINGS

An excellent first course for an elegant dinner or a main course for a luncheon.

---

3 cups chicken broth (or vegetable broth)

1 15.5-ounce can black beans, drained and rinsed

2 tablespoons water

1 tablespoon finely minced garlic

2 teaspoons ground cumin

pinch of kosher salt to taste

1 tablespoon chopped fresh cilantro

1 tablespoon fresh lime juice

¾ cup picked crabmeat (or 1 6-ounce can crabmeat)

2 tablespoons brandy (optional)

6 tablespoons sour cream

scallions, chopped (for garnish)

---

Heat the broth in a 2-quart saucepan.

In a food processor, purée the black beans, water, garlic, cumin, salt, cilantro, and lime juice until smooth.

Add the bean mixture to the heating broth and bring to a boil over medium heat.

Stir in the crabmeat and brandy and cook for an additional 2 to 3 minutes.

Ladle into 6 individual bowls and stir 1 tablespoon of sour cream into each serving; top with the chopped scallions.

Prepare for silence as your guests enjoy this delightful first course.

*Per serving:* calories 147, calories from fat 26, total fat 3 g, cholesterol 0 mg, carbohydrates 17 g, fiber 5 g, protein 8 g

# CUBAN BLACK BEAN SOUP

4 TO 6 SERVINGS

The Cuban black bean soup recipes I know could make up an entire cookbook of their own, so I have to include at least one version in this edition. So follows a rich and deliciously different black bean soup. The extra time this recipe takes is well worth the effort.

---

8 ounces dried black beans

6 cups chicken broth (or vegetable broth)

¾ cup diced onion

½ cup red bell pepper, seeded, diced, and puréed

2 teaspoons finely chopped garlic

½ teaspoon oregano

2 tablespoons dark rum

2 tablespoons lemon juice

1 cup fresh spinach, thinly sliced

salt and pepper to taste

sour cream (for garnish)

1 large tomato, diced

---

Rinse and soak the beans overnight in cold water.

Drain and rinse. Cover with the broth and bring to a boil. Reduce heat to simmer and cook until almost tender, about 1 hour. In a separate pan, stew onions, peppers, garlic, and oregano in a small amount of the stock until onions are tender. Add the onion mixture to the beans and continue to simmer for approximately 30 minutes more or until the beans are very tender. In a food processor or blender, purée one third of the bean soup until smooth. Return the purée to the pan with the whole bean soup. Stir in rum, lemon juice, spinach, salt, and pepper. Portion soup into large bowls and garnish with sour cream and diced tomatoes.

No matter what the variation, Cuban bread is a must, and a sliced avocado is heavenly.

*Per serving:* calories 180, calories from fat 32, total fat 4 g, cholesterol 6 mg, carbohydrate 22 g, fiber 7 g, protein 12 g

# BLACK BEAN MINESTRONE

4 SERVINGS

Minestrone, the all-time classic of Italian soups, is enhanced both in taste and in nutrition with the addition of the black bean. This recipe creates a hearty, soul-filling pottage that will not disappoint any minestrone aficionado.

1 large onion, thinly sliced

2 tablespoons olive oil

2 carrots, cut into ½-inch slices

½ head of cauliflower, cut into small flowerets

3 small zucchini, halved and cut into ¼-inch slices

4 cups chicken broth (or vegetable broth)

2 cups water

2 tablespoons minced garlic

2 15.5-ounce cans black beans, drained and rinsed

1 16-ounce can crushed tomatoes

1 head of escarole, well washed and cut up

In a large saucepan, cook the onion in oil over moderate heat, stirring, until golden. Add carrots and cauliflower and cook for 3 minutes, stirring occasionally. Add zucchini and cook for 3 minutes, again stirring occasionally. Add broth, water, garlic, and beans. Simmer for about 30 minutes. Stir in crushed tomatoes and escarole and cook another 30 minutes, until soup has thickened. Add salt and pepper to taste.

A minestrone is not complete without a healthy sprinkling of Parmesan cheese over the hot bowl. Adding hot garlic toast and a green salad makes this a perfect meal for a chilly afternoon or winter evening.

*Per serving:* calories 717, calories from fat 117, total fat 14 g, cholesterol 0 mg, carbohydrates 141 g, fiber 77 g, protein 37 g

# JOSÉ JESUS IGLASIAS'S MIMMA'S CUBAN BLACK BEANS 4 TO 6 SERVINGS

José was my partner in laughter, cooking, and dancing for many years. We had many fine arguments in the kitchen regarding technique and ingredients as we put together heavenly banquets for friends. This is his Mimma's recipe for the all-time Cuban staple.

José is gone now and Mimma is in Miami. Let their black beans and José's memory live forever! (José claimed later that he never put lime juice in his beans, but I remember he did, and it certainly belongs there.)

3 tablespoons olive oil

2 cloves garlic, minced (or more if you are a garlic hound)

4 15.5-ounce cans black beans, drained and rinsed

1 big splash mojo (approximately ¼ cup)

1 big splash Spanish cooking wine (approximately ¼ cup)

1 handful green olives with pimentos

juice of 1 lime

1 onion, finely chopped for topping

Heat olive oil in a large saucepan and add garlic. Brown garlic very lightly. Add beans, mojo, wine, and olives. Simmer for 30 minutes. Add lime juice (no matter what José said). Spoon over white rice and top with chopped onions. Serve with a dry white wine, an avocado salad, Cuban bread, and fried plantains. Oh José! Oh Mimma! Sooooo good.

*Per serving:* calories 290, calories from fat 67, total fat 8 g, cholesterol 0 mg, carbohydrates 42 g, fiber 15 g, protein 15 g

# BLACK BEAN CORN FRITTERS

25 FRITTERS

These are an absolute must at any barbecue or brunch with a Southwestern theme. Served warm with the tangy sauce, they disappear as quickly as popcorn.

---

1 8-ounce can whole kernel corn

small amount of milk, as needed (see below)

1½ cups flour

1 tablespoon baking powder

salt and black pepper to taste

1 egg, beaten

1 cup black beans, cooked, rinsed, well drained, and puréed in food processor until smooth

1 small can chopped green chilies

oil for deep frying

---

Drain corn; reserve the liquid. Add enough milk to the corn liquid to equal 1 cup. Stir together the dry ingredients. Combine egg, milk mixture, corn, beans, and chilies; Add to the dry ingredients. Mix just until moistened. Drop batter by tablespoonfuls into hot oil. Fry for about 2 minutes on each side or until golden. Drain on paper towels.

## Dipping Sauce

---

1 cup sour cream

hot sauce to taste

---

Mix together and top with chopped fresh cilantro.

Stand back and watch them disappear.

*Per serving:* calories 160, calories from fat 14, total fat 2 g, cholesterol 0 mg, carbohydrates 29 g, fiber 3 g, protein 6 g

# Main Dishes

. . . . . . . . . . . . . . . . . . . . . . . . . . . . . . .

## MARGIE MONTALVO'S PUERTO RICAN BLACK BEANS  4 SERVINGS

This is from the kitchen of a wonderful friend, a dinner that comforts and fills. Margie always has something delicious on her table, and this dish in particular is a favorite of her family. Margie does not measure, so you don't have to either; the amounts are approximate.

---

2 tablespoons olive oil

½ cup chopped green peppers

½ cup chopped onions

1 tablespoon minced garlic

1 15.5-ounce can black beans, drained and rinsed

1½ cans of water (using the bean can for a measure)

½ cup tomato sauce

1 potato, cut into cubes

1 2-inch-wide slice pumpkin, peeled and cut into cubes (or ½ acorn squash, cubed)

salt to taste

---

Heat oil in a medium-size saucepan and sauté peppers, onions, and garlic until soft. Add beans, water, tomato sauce, potato, and pumpkin. Bring to a boil, reduce heat, and simmer for about 20 minutes until potatoes and pumpkin are soft.

Margie traditionally serves this over white rice, with a crisp green salad on the side. The addition of tostones (fried green plantains) completes the picture perfectly.

*Per serving:* calories 456, calories from fat 69, total fat 8 g, cholesterol 0, carbohydrates 93 g, fiber 27 g, protein 14 g

# SPICY BLACK BEAN PIZZA

16 SLICES

Move over, pepperoni. This is dedicated to all of those who feel that eating healthy is no fun and gone are the days of pizza and beer. Well, I give you pizza. The beer is up to you.

2 10-ounce cans black beans, drained and rinsed

9 plum tomatoes, chopped

1 cup cilantro leaves, chopped

hot sauce, such as Tabasco or Texas Pete, to taste

1 teaspoon chopped garlic (or more!)

juice of 1 ½ limes

2 cups shredded cheddar cheese

2 cups shredded Monterey Jack cheese

2 prepared pizza crusts, such as Boboli brand

1 cup chopped scallions

Preheat oven to 450° F.

In a bowl, combine black beans, tomatoes, cilantro, hot sauce, garlic, and lime juice. Combine both cheeses in another small bowl.

Place pizza crusts on a baking sheet. Divide the black bean mixture into two equal parts and spread mixture evenly on the pizza crusts.

Divide cheese mixture and sprinkle evenly over the tops of both pizzas.

Bake for 10 minutes or until cheese is melted. Remove from oven and sprinkle ½ cup scallions on each pizza.

Do whatever you do on pizza-and-beer nights.

*Per serving:* calories 270, calories from fat 120, total fat 14 g, cholesterol 41 mg, carbohydrates 16 g, fiber 6 g, protein 21 g

# BLACK BEAN CURRY

4 SERVINGS

And why not? Just don't leave out the fresh cilantro.

2 tablespoons olive oil

1 clove garlic, minced

1 medium onion, chopped

1 green pepper, chopped

1 tomato, chopped

2 tablespoons curry powder

2 15.5-ounce cans black beans, drained and rinsed

¼ cup chicken broth (or water)

1 tablespoon lemon juice

3 tablespoons chopped fresh cilantro

## Condiments

peanuts

coconut

raisins

chopped scallions

Sauté garlic, onion, pepper, and tomato in oil until soft. Add the curry powder and stir.

Add beans, broth, and lemon juice and simmer for 15 minutes. Just before serving, stir in the cilantro.

Serve over fluffy basmati rice. Top with whatever combination of condiments you prefer.

*Per serving:* calories 311, calories from fat 73, total fat 8 g, cholesterol 0 mg, carbohydrates 46 g, fiber 17 g, protein 15 g

# BLACK-HEARTED CHILI

6 SERVINGS

This chili has a twist. A little different, a lot of flavor, spicy yet sweet.

---

1 medium onion, chopped

2 small zucchini, cut into ½-inch pieces

2 carrots, sliced into ¼-inch pieces

2 celery stalks, sliced into ¼-inch pieces

1 28-ounce can crushed tomatoes with Italian herbs (undrained)

½ cup chopped fresh pineapple (the twist and the sweetness)

2 15.5-ounce cans black beans, drained and rinsed

3 tablespoons chili powder

2 teaspoons ground cumin

---

Combine all ingredients in a large saucepan over medium-low heat. Bring to a simmer and cook for 30 minutes, uncovered, stirring occasionally.

Serve in a heavy bowl, topped with a dollop of sour cream. Wait! Some chopped scallions, too.

Cornbread just happens to go well with all good chilis.

*Per serving:* calories 872, calories from fat 62, total fat 7 g, cholesterol 0 mg, carbohydrates 191 g, fiber 53 g, protein 46 g

# BLACK BEAN CHILI WITH SHERRY

4 SERVINGS

Yes, you can feed guests or family a hearty dinner with less than one hour prep time. This recipe is easily doubled or tripled for a crowd.

2 15.5-ounce cans black beans

2 medium onions, chopped

2 jalapeño chilies, chopped and seeded

4 tomatoes, chopped

⅔ cup dry cooking sherry

4 cloves garlic, crushed

1 tablespoon chili powder

1 teaspoon salt

1 teaspoon ground cumin

black pepper to taste

3 ounces shredded cheddar cheese

3 ounces shredded Monterey Jack cheese

Drain and rinse the black beans and put in a medium-size heavy pot. Add onions, chilies, tomatoes, sherry, garlic, chili powder, salt, cumin, and black pepper. Stir well and bring to a gentle boil. Reduce the heat to low and simmer for 30 minutes, stirring occasionally. If the mixture gets too dry, add more sherry.

As with all good chili, top with the shredded cheese after ladling into bowls.

*Per serving:* calories 390, calories from fat 5, total fat 7 g, cholesterol 16 mg, carbohydrates 51 g, fiber 17 g, protein 24 g

# HUEVOS RANCHEROS WITH BLACK BEANS

4 SERVINGS

It's supposed to be a breakfast, but this version of the classic cowboy favorite becomes hearty enough for dinner with the addition of black beans.

2 teaspoons canola oil

2 green peppers, cut into strips

1 cup thinly sliced red onion

2 jalapeño peppers, seeded and minced

1 14.5-ounce can diced tomatoes

1 15.5-ounce can black beans, drained and rinsed

2 teaspoons balsamic vinegar

1 teaspoon ground cumin

1 tablespoon finely chopped cilantro

½ teaspoon salt

4 medium (8-inch) corn tortillas

4 eggs

1 cup shredded cheddar cheese

Heat oil in a large nonstick skillet. Add green pepper, onion, and jalapeños and cook for 2 minutes. Stir in tomatoes, beans, vinegar, cumin, cilantro, and salt and cook 5 minutes or until mixture is heated through and vegetables are soft.

Spray a medium-sized nonstick skillet with cooking spray and heat over medium heat. Add the corn tortillas one at a time and warm for 1 minute on each side. Remove from skillet and cover to keep warm.

Remove the skillet from the heat and spray again with the cooking spray. Heat again over medium heat, add whole eggs, and cook until whites begin to set, about 2 minutes. Gently flip the eggs, leaving yolks intact. Sprinkle with the cheese, cover pan, and cook for approximately 1 minute or until cheese is melted.

Place a corn tortilla on each plate, top with the bean mixture, and place an egg, cheese side up, on top.

A dollop of guacamole on the side is a good addition to this comfortable dish.

*Per serving:* calories 962, calories from fat 219, total fat 25 g, cholesterol 281 mg, carbohydrates 160 g, fiber 41 g, protein 52 g

# SPIRALS WITH BLACK BEAN SALSA AND GRAPE TOMATOES 4 SERVINGS

This dish is quick, nutritious, and pleasing to both the eye and the palate.

---

8 ounces uncooked spiral macaroni (e.g., rotelle or rotini)

2 tablespoons olive oil

1 bunch scallions, thinly sliced (both green and white parts)

1½ teaspoons ground cumin

2 tablespoons fresh lime juice

1 15.5-ounce can black beans, drained and rinsed

salt to taste

freshly ground black pepper to taste

10 grape tomatoes, halved

3 tablespoons chopped fresh cilantro

---

Cook the spiral macaroni according to the package instructions.

While pasta is cooking, heat the oil in a medium saucepan over medium heat. Add scallions and cumin and cook for 2 minutes. Remove from heat and stir in lime juice. Add beans, salt, and pepper; toss to coat.

Just before draining the pasta, measure ½ cup of the cooking water into the black bean salsa mixture. Drain the pasta, return it to the pot, and add the bean mixture. Cook over medium heat until the sauce is boiling and thick enough to coat the pasta. Remove from heat and stir in the tomatoes. Serve immediately and top with the cilantro.

*Per serving:* calories 220, calories from fat 96, total fat 11 g, cholesterol 9 mg, carbohydrates 31 g, fiber 9 g, protein 12 g

# BLACK BEAN BURRITOS

6 SERVINGS

What's wonderful about these burritos is that you can completely satisfy your craving for Mexican food and not miss the meat. This recipe has provided a theme night dinner on many an occasion. Add a pitcher of margaritas, and you're gold!

2 15.5-ounce cans black beans, drained and rinsed

1 tablespoon vegetable oil

1 medium onion, chopped

1 tablespoon minced garlic

1 4-ounce can chopped green chilies

¾ cup medium or hot taco sauce

6 large (10-inch) flour tortillas

1 cup Monterey Jack cheese, shredded

1 cup sharp cheddar cheese, shredded

1½–2 cups shredded lettuce

6 tablespoons sour cream

1 large tomato, diced

4 scallions, chopped

1 cup sliced black olives

Preheat oven to 350° F.

Mash beans in a medium-sized bowl. In a large skillet, cook onions and garlic in vegetable oil until onions are soft. Add the mashed beans, green chilies, and taco sauce and stir until evenly mixed and heated through.

Heat tortillas either by placing in a hot fry pan for approximately 1 minute or by wrapping tortillas flat in aluminum foil and placing them in the oven as it preheats for about 5 minutes.

Spread bean mixture over the tortillas and roll up. Place in a baking dish and top with both cheeses.

Bake for 20 to 25 minutes or until cheese is melted and starts to bubble.

Serve topped with lettuce, a dollop of sour cream, diced tomatoes, scallions, and black olives.

*Per serving:* calories 436, calories from fat 140, total fat 16 g, cholesterol 33 mg, carbohydrates 50 g, fiber 11 g, protein 25 g

# BLACK BEAN PANCAKES

4 SERVINGS

The batter for this high-fiber, high-protein breakfast can be made the night before. Even if you have a rough time just getting to the kitchen in the morning, this breakfast will give you an energy boost that will last well past lunchtime.

---

1 15.5-ounce can black beans, drained and rinsed

2 tablespoons water

2 egg whites

1 teaspoon vanilla

4 tablespoons sugar (or 4 tablespoons Splenda)

½ cup flour

½ cup milk

1 tablespoon vegetable or canola oil

nonstick cooking spray

---

Place beans and water into a food processor and purée until smooth. Use only 1 cup of the purée and put aside the rest for use in some other recipe. (Puréed black beans can be used as a thickening agent in any of the soups or a head start for the black bean dip.)

To the 1 cup of bean purée, add egg whites, vanilla, sugar, flour, and milk.

Blend in the food processor until smooth.

Refrigerate for at least 2 hours or as long as overnight.

Coat a large nonstick skillet with cooking spray and preheat over medium heat. For each pancake, spoon 2 tablespoons of batter into skillet and cook until bubbles break on the pancake surface. Turn and cook until lightly browned on the other side. (If the batter becomes too thick, thin with milk.) Keep warm in a low oven.

Makes 16 small pancakes. Top with the following sauce.

## Topping

---

½ cup sour cream

1 tablespoon brown sugar (or 2 drops liquid stevia or 1 tablespoon Splenda)

sprinkle of cinnamon

---

Mix above ingredients together and spoon over the pancakes.

Serve with fresh strawberries and mint if desired.

*Per serving:* calories 293, calories from fat 42, total fat 5 g, cholesterol 14 mg, carbohydrates 51 g, fiber 8 g, protein 13 g

# BRAZILIAN BLACK BEANS

6 SERVINGS

This unique tropical dish can be treated like curry: Supply the condiments in dishes on the side and let the happy eaters top the beans with whatever appeals to their tastebuds.

2 tablespoons olive oil

1 onion, diced

1 green bell pepper, chopped

1 yellow pepper, chopped

1 tablespoon minced garlic

2 15.5-ounce cans black beans, drained and rinsed

1 tablespoon fresh lemon juice

2 tablespoons frozen orange juice concentrate

3 tomatoes, chopped

3 teaspoons ground cumin

up to 1 cup tomato juice

2 tablespoons black rum

In a large skillet, heat the olive oil; add the onion and sauté until soft (about 3 minutes). Stir in peppers and garlic; sauté for 3 more minutes. Add beans, lemon juice, orange juice, tomatoes, and cumin. Cover and simmer on low heat for about 5 minutes. If the mixture gets too thick, add the tomato juice to thin as needed.

Remove one cup of the bean mixture; combine with the rum and purée until smooth. Return the puréed beans to the skillet; stir and simmer for 20 minutes.

Serve over fluffy rice and have several condiments available in pretty dishes for topping choices. Try these: chopped scallions (both white and green parts), chopped tomatoes, chopped green chilies, thinly sliced bananas, tostones (fried green plantain slices), orange sections, cut into 3 pieces each, unsweetened coconut flakes.

*Per serving (less toppings):* calories 252, calories from fat 48, total fat 6 g, cholesterol 0 mg, carbohydrates 39 g, fiber 12 g, protein 12 g

# Desserts

. . . . . . . . . . . . . . . . . . . . . . . . . . .

## BLACK BEAN ALMONDINE FLAN

8 SERVINGS

This recipe is more than just a little special. Not only is it the first bean flan in the history of flans, but it was created, with love, especially for this book by Eugenio Concepción Sepúlveda of Boqueron, Puerto Rico. An excellent chef, Eugene took on the challenge of this creation with the same enthusiasm he puts into our friendship.

---

1 15.5-ounce can black beans, drained and rinsed

1 13.5-ounce can coconut milk

1 8-ounce package of cream cheese or low-fat cream cheese

6 eggs

3 tablespoons vanilla

5 small envelopes Splenda

½ cup sliced toasted almonds soaked in ½ cup Amaretto or Frangelico liquor

nonstick vegetable spray

---

Preheat oven to 350° F.

Blend beans, coconut milk, cream cheese, eggs, vanilla, and Splenda in a food processor or blender until smooth.

Coat a 9-inch glass pie plate with non-stick spray. Pour batter into the pie plate.

Place pie plate with batter into a larger pan containing water.

Place in preheated oven and cook for 45 to 60 minutes, depending on your oven, until set. Test this by inserting a knife into the flan—if it comes out clean, the flan is done.

Let cool for 15 minutes. Invert the flan onto a platter and spoon the toasted sliced almonds over the top. Pour remaining liquor over the top of the entire flan.

Serve with a dollop of whipped cream and a sliced strawberry or two with a mint leaf on the side.

This has been tested on the most skeptical of flan lovers and passed with extraordinary reviews.

Enjoy.

*Per serving:* calories 353, calories from fat 180, total fat 21 g, cholesterol 187 mg, carbohydrates 16 g, fiber 5 g, protein 16 g

# HEAVENLY CHOCOLATE ALMOND RASPBERRY BLACK BEAN TORTE  8 SERVINGS

Whew, what a name! It's almost as big as the taste! This is a simply elegant, delicious dessert that you can confidently serve at a dinner party. I love not telling people it is made of beans until they "aahhhh" over their first serving.

1 15.5-ounce can black beans

½ cup of margarine

1 cup sugar (or 3 teaspoons stevia powder or 1 cup Splenda)

3 eggs, separated

6 tablespoons cocoa

2 teaspoons almond extract or 1 tablespoon Amaretto liquor

⅓ cup slivered almonds

(Right, there is no flour.)

Preheat oven to 350° F.

Drain and rinse the beans. Purée in a food processor with a tablespoon of water to make it creamy. Hold aside.

Beat margarine and sugar or sweetener well. Beat in egg yolks, one at a time. Add cocoa, almond flavoring, bean purée, and almonds. Mix until blended.

In a separate bowl, beat egg whites until stiff peaks form. Gently fold the beaten whites into the batter.

Pour into a greased 8-inch round cake pan. Bake for 1 hour.

Cool and top with raspberry topping and almond whipped cream.

Garnish with fresh raspberries and mint leaves.

## Raspberry topping

1 quart fresh or frozen raspberries

¼ cup sugar (or ⅓ teaspoon stevia powder or ¼ cup Splenda)

1 tablespoon corn starch

Mix raspberries, sweetener, and corn-starch in a small saucepan.

Heat until bubbling, reduce heat to low, and simmer for about 10 minutes until thickened. Let cool.

## Almond whipped cream

1 pint heavy cream

1 teaspoon almond extract

Whip until thickened and cream peaks.

A perfect ending with perhaps a cordial of Amaretto and coffee.

*Per serving:* calories 329, calories from fat 154, total fat 17 g, cholesterol 105 mg, carbohydrates 38 g, fiber 6 g, protein 8 g

# DOUBLE CHOCOLATE WALNUT BLACK BEAN BREAD

2 LOAVES (16 SLICES)

To the unsuspecting dinner guest or casual snacker, this chocolaty treat is just a wonderfully rich and delicious chocolate dessert bread. No one has to know that this is beans at their best.

---

1 cup canola oil

1½ cups brown sugar (or 2 teaspoons stevia powder or 1½ cups Splenda)

4 eggs (lightly beaten)

2 teaspoons vanilla

1 cup cocoa

1 teaspoon baking soda

1 teaspoon baking powder

1½ cups flour

½ cup chopped walnuts

1 cup chocolate or carob chips

2 15.5-ounce cans black beans, drained, rinsed, and puréed

---

Preheat oven to 350° F.

In a large bowl, whisk together the oil and brown sugar. Beat in the eggs. Add vanilla, cocoa, baking soda, baking powder, and flour. Fold in the walnuts and chocolate chips.

Add puréed beans, mixing well.

Pour batter into two 8-inch greased loaf pans. Bake for 45 minutes or until a knife inserted in the center comes out clean. Then, while it's still warm, eat it. Perhaps after dinner or before bed, perhaps with milk or a nice espresso with a little lemon twist?

*Per slice:* calories 401, calories from fat 188, total fat 22 g, cholesterol 62 mg, carbohydrates 48 g, fiber 7 g, protein 9 g

# BIG, BAD BLACK BEAN BROWNIES

12 SQUARES

Brownies? Beans? Yes!

---

½ cup margarine

2 cups sugar (or 2 teaspoons stevia powder or 2 cups Splenda)

6 tablespoons cocoa

1 tablespoon instant coffee powder

4 eggs

1 cup puréed black beans (made from 1 15.5-ounce can black beans, drained and rinsed)

¾ cup chopped walnuts (optional)

P.S. No, I did not forget the flour: there is none.

---

Preheat oven to 350° F.

Beat together margarine, sugar, cocoa, and coffee. Add eggs, one at a time, beating between additions. Beat in bean purée. Stir in nuts. Pour batter into a 9 x 13-inch greased pan.

Bake for 45 to 50 minutes.

Cool completely and cut into squares.

Drink milk with these!!

*Per serving:* calories 300, calories from fat 130, total fat 15 g, cholesterol 90 mg, carbohydrates 40 g, fiber 3 g, protein 5 g

# CHOCOLATE WALNUT BEAN TRUFFLES (A CANDY)

14 TRUFFLES

These crunchy, chocolaty, healthful little bites will astound all.

---

1 ½ cup black beans, mashed well

1 pound confectioner's sugar, sifted

1 teaspoon vanilla extract

1 cup chopped walnuts

¼ cup butter, melted

1 ½ cup chocolate chips

2 tablespoons paraffin wax

---

Combine the black beans, confectioner's sugar, vanilla, nuts, and butter. Roll into balls the size of a walnut. Place on a waxed paper-covered cookie sheet and chill for 1 hour.

Melt the chocolate chips with the paraffin. Dip the balls into the chocolate while it is still warm. Put them back on the waxed paper-covered cookie sheet and chill again to set the chocolate.

*Per serving:* calories 115, calories from fat 70, total fat 8 g, cholesterol 5 mg, carbohydrates 10 g, fiber 2 g, protein 2 g

# CHOCOLATE ALMOND BLACK BEAN CHEESECAKE

12 SERVINGS

What can I say? Rich, creamy, sinful—this will live up to all your cheesecake expectations.

## Crust

1¼ cups graham cracker crumbs

½ cup toasted almonds, ground in food processor

¼ cup sugar (or ¼ cup Splenda)

½ cup melted butter

Preheat oven to 300° F.

## Filling

1 15.5-ounce can black beans, drained and rinsed

2 tablespoons water

3 8-ounce packages cream cheese, softened

6 eggs

3 tablespoons cocoa

1 cup sugar (or 1 cup Splenda)

2 tablespoons almond extract

1 teaspoon vanilla

Combine the ingredients for the crust and press into a 9-inch springform pan. Cover the bottom and at least 1 inch up the sides with the graham cracker mixture.

Put the drained beans into a food processor or blender and purée until very smooth. If necessary, add 1 to 2 tablespoons of water.

In a large bowl, beat cream cheese until fluffy. Stir in puréed black beans. Add eggs one at a time, beating after each egg. Beat in remaining ingredients.

Pour filling mixture into the prepared springform pan.

Bake until center is set and a sharp knife inserted halfway between center and edge comes out clean, about 1 hour. Cool to room temperature on a wire rack. Refrigerate overnight.

Excellent served as is, or you can get decorative and add whipped cream, sliced almonds, fruit, or whatever appeals.

*Per serving:* calories 468, calories from fat 299, total fat 34 g, cholesterol 206 mg, carbohydrates 31 g, fiber 4 g, protein 12 g

# FAKE' EM OUT FUDGE

ABOUT 30 SQUARES

This is real fudge—every gooey, delicious bite. No one will ever think to ask what type of beans are starring in this delight!

---

1 cup cooked black beans, rinsed

¾ cup melted butter

¾ cup cocoa

2 tablespoons vanilla

2 pounds powdered sugar

½ cup chopped walnuts

---

Mash or purée the black beans in a food processor. Add the melted butter, cocoa, and vanilla, stirring to mix well.

Stir in the sugar and the walnuts.

Spread into a greased 9 x 13-inch pan. Put the pan in the refrigerator; let chill for at least an hour. Cut into 30 squares and store right up front in the refrigerator for the refrigerator-gazers to spot easily when they stand there with door open, peering in for the perfect snack.

*Per square:* calories 138, calories from fat 108, total fat 12 g, cholesterol 25 mg, carbohydrates 6 g, fiber 3 g, protein 3 g

# White Beans

# White Beans

## Great Northern · Navy · Cannellini

*W*hite *beans include great northern,* navy, and cannellini. In most any recipe, these three varieties are almost always interchangeable.

Great northern beans are the dried seeds of mature green beans. These medium-size beans originated in northern Europe and are traditionally used in the United States in the famous "Boston Baked Beans." In France, they are most often found in the popular cassoulet. Though rather bland on their own, great northern beans can act as a flavor sponge, soaking up the combined flavors of the foods they are cooked with. Thanks to the anonymity of their flavor, you can easily sneak great northerns (and the nutrition they provide) into almost any type of recipe, especially desserts.

The cannellini is the most popular bean in Italy. It is one of the larger beans and is sometimes referred to as a white kidney bean because of its similarity in shape and size to the red kidney bean. This creamy white bean has a very mellow taste and maintains its shape nicely when cooked.

As with its fellow white beans, the navy bean originally hails from Europe. Currently, over five billion pounds are grown in the United States each year. It is the smallest of the white beans—about the size of a green pea——but with more of an oval shape. Almost a miniature version of the great northern bean, the navy bean has the same ability to take on any flavor, as its own is very mild.

## Nutritional values for 1 cup of cooked beans

### Great Northern Beans

Calories 209   Protein 14.7 g   Carbohydrates 37.3 g   Total Fat 0.79 g   Fiber 12.4 g
Iron 3.7 mg   Magnesium 88.5 mg   Folate 181 mcg   Calcium 120 mg

### Cannellini Beans

Calories 225   Protein 15.3 g   Carbohydrates 40.4 g   Total Fat 0.88 g   Fiber 11.3 g
Iron 5.2 mg   Magnesium 80 mg   Folate 229 mcg

### Navy Beans

Calories 258   Protein 15.8 g   Carbohydrates 47.8 g   Total Fat 1.0 g   Fiber 11.6 g
Iron 4.5 mg   Folate 255 mcg   Calcium 128 mg

## APPETIZERS

White Bean and Red Pepper Spread
Pesto and Bean White Pizza
White Bean and Avocado Salsa
White Bean Purée
White Bean and Green Onion
  Pancakes

## SALADS, SOUPS & SIDES

Two Bean and Broccoli Salad
White Beans and Red Cabbage
Tuna and White Bean Salad
Green and White Salad
White Bean Salad with Wilted Escarole
White Bean Minestrone
White Bean and Avocado Gazpacho
Zuppa di Fagioli alla Toscana
Two Pasta and Bean Soup
Barbeque Beans
Boston Baked Beans
Oriental Beans
Vegetable and White Bean Roast
Barbunyali Plaki

## MAIN DISHES

Pasta with Asparagus, Butter Beans,
  and Caramelized Onions
White Beans Niçoises
Florentine Beans and Pasta
Tortellini with Escarole and Beans
Portobello, Bean, and Cheese Open-
  Face Sandwiches
From the Land of Milk and Honey
Curried Bean Sandwich Spread
Pasta e Fagioli
Escarole e Fagioli
Pasta Fagiole II—alla Petrina
White Bean-Stuffed Acorn Squash
Pasta with Beans, Basil, and Corn
Gnocchi
Pasta Puttanesca with Cannellini Beans
Tomato and White Bean Casserole

## DESSERTS

Coconut Custard
Chocolate-Covered "Marzipan"
Oatmeal Chocolate Chip Cookies
Pumpkin Almond Oat Muffins
White Bean and Banana Breakfast
  Fritters
The Great Maple Walnut Banana Bean
  Bread
Bean, I Mean, **Cream** Puffs
Pie Crust

# Appetizers

## WHITE BEAN AND RED PEPPER SPREAD

6 SERVINGS

This dip has an attractive color and delicious, fresh taste. Great as a crudités dip or excellent on toasted pita triangles.

---

1 15.5-ounce can great northern beans, drained and rinsed

½ cup finely chopped sweet red peppers, plus extra for garnish

2 tablespoons chopped scallions (both white and green parts)

2–3 sprigs fresh parsley, chopped

---

Place beans and red peppers in a food processor and process until smooth, adding 1 to 2 tablespoons water as needed to facilitate blending.

Stir in the scallions. Place in a dip bowl; garnish with parsley and extra chopped red peppers.

This spread can be prepared in a matter of minutes, so it's a great dish to bring to a party when time is something you don't have. In the right bowl, with the right garnish, this is a magazine-quality presentation.

*Per serving:* calories 211, calories from fat 6, total fat 1 g, cholesterol 39 mg, carbohydrates 39 g, fiber 13 g, protein 13 g

# PESTO AND BEAN WHITE PIZZA

8 SLICES

This snack not only provides an excellent use for all that wonderful summertime abundance of fresh basil, but is an extraordinary combination of flavors never before found in a pizza.

---

1 prepared pizza shell, such as Boboli

1 10-ounce can cannellini beans, drained and rinsed

2 tablespoons water

1 cup fresh parsley leaves

1 cup fresh basil leaves

1 tablespoon minced garlic

¼ cup chicken broth (or vegetable broth)

4 tablespoons grated Parmesan cheese (divided use)

1½ tablespoons olive oil

1½ cups ricotta cheese

4½ ounces mozzarella cheese, shredded

2 tablespoons milk

4 large plum tomatoes, thinly sliced

---

Preheat oven to 450° F.

Spray a 12-inch pizza pan with non-stick cooking spray. Place pizza shell on the pan.

Place beans in a food processor with 2 tablespoons water and process until almost smooth, but still slightly lumpy. Spread the bean mixture evenly over the pizza shell, leaving a 1-inch border all around.

To make the pesto, combine parsley, basil, and garlic in a food processor and process until finely chopped. Add the broth, 2 tablespoons of the Parmesan cheese, and the olive oil. Process until well mixed. Spread the pesto evenly over the bean mixture on the pizza shell.

In a separate bowl, combine ricotta, mozzarella, milk, and the remaining 2 tablespoons of Parmesan cheese. Top the pizza evenly with the cheese mixture and arrange the tomato slices over the cheese.

Bake 20 to 25 minutes or until cheese is melted and bubbling.

Serve immediately. Feel free to make 2 or 3 of these, since you won't be able to stop at just one slice and your guests won't either.

*Per serving:* calories 413, calories from fat 106, total fat 12 g, cholesterol 26 mg, carbohydrates 52 g, fiber 6 g, protein 24 g

# WHITE BEAN AND AVOCADO SALSA

6 SERVINGS

This is a colorful, flavorful, and high-fiber twist on a great dip for chips. Quick and easy, this makes a wonderful party or buffet dish.

---

1 cup navy beans, drained and rinsed

2 firm ripe avocados, peeled and diced

2 fresh, preferably vine-ripened, tomatoes, diced small

1 red onion, diced

4 tablespoons fresh lime juice

2 teaspoons olive oil

3 tablespoons fresh chopped cilantro

salt to taste (optional)

---

Gently stir together all ingredients. Cover with a plastic wrap and allow flavors to blend for at least an hour.

Serve with large white corn chips.

*Per serving:* calories 175, calories from fat 100, total fat 12 g, cholesterol 0 mg, carbohydrates 16 g, fiber 6 g, protein 4 g

# WHITE BEAN PURÉE

6 TO 8 SERVINGS

My sister Lucille, who has been a bean eater for years, created this wonderfully different bean dish. Not only is it a great crudité dip, but she also uses it as a "mayonnaise" on sandwiches. This mixture is also excellent when drizzled over other vegetable dishes, such as cooked spinach, mashed potatoes, or broccoli.

1 15-ounce can cannellini beans, drained and rinsed

grated rind of 1 whole lemon

1 clove finely minced garlic

1 splash olive oil

1 teaspoon fresh rosemary (or ½ teaspoon dried)

freshly ground black pepper to taste

Place all ingredients except the olive oil in a food processor. As you process the mixture, slowly drizzle in the olive oil. The more you add, the fluffier the purée will be.

What you choose to use this with is as limitless as your imagination. Always top with some fresh parsley, just because.

*Per serving:* calories 268, calories from fat 45, total fat 5 g, cholesterol 0 mg, carbohydrates 42 g, fiber 10 g, protein 16 g

# WHITE BEAN AND GREEN ONION PANCAKES

6 TO 8 SERVINGS

This is a thoroughly different appetizer that can also be served as a side dish with a salad or vegetable. Great with grilled fish, too.

3 cups cooked cannellini beans, drained and rinsed

1 teaspoon white wine vinegar

2 eggs

1 tablespoon vegetable oil

1 teaspoon baking powder

5 scallions, thinly sliced (both white and green parts)

3 teaspoons corn oil

2–3 sprigs fresh parsley, chopped

Purée the beans, vinegar, eggs, vegetable oil, and baking powder in a food processor until smooth. Pour into a medium-size bowl. Add scallions, reserving 2 tablespoons of the onions.

Heat the corn oil over a medium-high heat in a large skillet. Drop the batter by 2 tablespoons for each pancake into the hot oil. Fry until the underside is a golden brown and flip to fry the other side until golden.

## Sauce

1 teaspoon white wine vinegar

5 tablespoons melted unsalted butter

1 teaspoon dry mustard

1 tablespoon tamari or soy sauce

Whisk together the sauce ingredients to blend well.

Arrange the pancakes on a large platter. Drizzle the sauce evenly over the pancakes. Sprinkle the reserved chopped scallions and the fresh parsley over the top.

*Per serving:* calories 397, calories from fat 136, total fat 15 g, cholesterol 86 mg, carbohydrates 47 g, fiber 12 g, protein 20 g

# Salads, Soups & Sides

## TWO BEAN AND BROCCOLI SALAD

The freshness of the vegetables and herbs in this recipe lend a light, summery impression to a very healthful, hearty meal.

---

1 cup small broccoli florets

1 cup crisp green beans, cleaned and cut into ½-inch pieces

1 15.5-ounce can cannellini beans, drained and rinsed

1 small onion, chopped fine

½ cup diced green pepper

⅓ cup olive oil

3 tablespoons balsamic vinegar

1 tablespoon minced garlic

1 teaspoon sugar

3 tablespoons chopped fresh parsley

1 tablespoon chopped fresh basil

---

Boil or steam the broccoli florets and the green beans separately until crisp-tender. Drain in a colander and rinse with cold water. Mix the green beans and broccoli with the white beans, onion, and green pepper.

Whisk together the oil, vinegar, garlic, and sugar. Pour over the vegetable mixture; add the parsley and fresh basil and toss well.

Refrigerate for at least 4 hours to overnight for maximum flavor.

This white and green, fresh-looking and fresh-tasting salad can be served over curly green lettuce. If you prefer a little extra color, add some grape tomatoes or cherry tomatoes around the edges.

Serve as a summertime side or add bread and wine and make it a full lunch.

*Per serving:* calories 566, calories from fat 169, total fat 19 g, cholesterol 0 mg, carbohydrates 76 g, fiber 19 g, protein 27 g

# WHITE BEANS AND RED CABBAGE

6 SERVINGS

This delightfully different and colorful recipe came from a "what to do with red cabbage?" series, but the beans are the first ingredient and so...

---

2 15.5-ounce cans navy beans, drained and rinsed

2 tablespoons vegetable oil

2 cups cooked brown basmati rice

2–3 tablespoons balsamic vinegar

½ medium-size red cabbage, shredded and diced

½ large Vidalia onion, diced

½ cup diced figs (about 4 fresh figs, or use an apple)

2 teaspoons cinnamon

---

Mash one can of the navy beans and leave the other can whole. Heat oil in a large saucepan and add beans, both mashed and whole. Stir until heated through.

Add the cooked basmati rice to the beans.

In a large skillet, heat balsamic vinegar and add the shredded red cabbage, onions, and figs; sauté until cabbage is soft.

Add to the bean mixture and stir well.

Spice with the cinnamon.

*Per serving:* calories 225, calories from fat 48, total fat 5 g, cholesterol 0 mg, carbohydrates 35 g, fiber 9 g, protein 11 g

# TUNA AND WHITE BEAN SALAD

4 SERVINGS

Extremely high in protein, this nicely colored and flavorful dish makes for the perfect lunch—either sit-down or brown-bag style.

---

1 15.5-ounce can cannellini beans, drained and rinsed

1 12-ounce can chunk white tuna in water, drained

1 cup celery, finely chopped

½ cup diced red onion

¼ cup diced green bell pepper

½ cup finely chopped fresh parsley

1 4-ounce jar roasted red peppers, drained and chopped

---

Combine the above ingredients in a large bowl. Gently toss with the following vinaigrette without breaking the beans.

## Vinaigrette

---

2 tablespoons balsamic vinegar

4 tablespoons extra virgin olive oil

1 tablespoon canola oil

½ teaspoon finely minced garlic

1 teaspoon sugar or Splenda

sea salt and freshly ground pepper to taste

---

Whisk together the above ingredients and pour over the salad.

Chill.

Serve this on a glass dish with a large leaf of curly lettuce. Divide the salad into 4 parts and spoon over the lettuce. If desired, sprinkle some black olives and sliced tomatoes on the sides of the dish along with some extra sprigs of curly parsley.

*Per serving:* calories 416, calories from fat 40, total fat 5 g, cholesterol 0 mg, carbohydrates 71 g, fiber 18 g, protein 26 g

# GREEN AND WHITE SALAD

6 TO 8 SERVINGS

This vibrant salad is a lead-in to spring when fresh green beans become available. (If it's not spring, thaw frozen green beans and use them raw from the package.)

---

¼ cup olive oil

2 tablespoons lemon juice

2 teaspoons Dijon mustard

sea salt and fresh ground pepper to taste

1 15.5-ounce can great northern beans, drained and rinsed

4 cups green beans, sliced into 1-inch pieces

½ cup chopped fresh parsley

3 shallots, minced

2 teaspoons chopped fresh basil

---

Whisk together the olive oil, lemon juice, mustard, salt, and pepper. Combine with great northern beans and green beans, parsley, shallots, and basil in a large bowl. Stir thoroughly but gently to blend flavors. Let sit for at least one hour before serving.

Thinly sliced carrots around the edge of the serving provide a vibrant color contrast.

*Per serving:* calories 237, calories from fat 65, total fat 7 g, cholesterol 0 mg, carbohydrates 34 g, fiber 11 g, protein 11 g

# WHITE BEAN SALAD WITH WILTED ESCAROLE

6 TO 8 SERVINGS

This wonderfully garlicky salad could be a first course, a side dish, or a great lunch all on its own. Keep in mind, there is no such thing as too much garlic.

---

¼ cup plus 3 tablespoons extra virgin olive oil (divided use)

6–8 cloves garlic, thinly sliced

¼ cup lemon juice

2 cups dried cannellini beans or 5 cups canned cannellini beans, drained and rinsed

2 heads escarole

kosher salt and freshly ground black pepper to taste

¼ cup chopped flat-leaf parsley

1 lemon, cut into wedges

---

Combine ¼ cup of the olive oil with the garlic in a small saucepan and cook over medium heat approximately 5 minutes or until the garlic is golden, taking care not to burn the garlic. Transfer oil and garlic to a small bowl; add the lemon juice and stir. Pour over cooked beans and set aside.

Cut escarole heads into quarters and rinse well. Heat a large skillet. Brush the escarole with the remaining 3 tablespoons of olive oil, season with the salt and pepper, and cook on high heat, turning once, until leaves are wilted and slightly brown. Transfer to a platter and top with the bean mixture.

Sprinkle with the chopped parsley and serve garnished with lemon wedges.

*Per serving:* calories 489, calories from fat 69, total fat 8 g, cholesterol 0 mg, carbohydrates 71 g, fiber 19 g, protein 30 g

# WHITE BEAN MINESTRONE

8 SERVINGS

This comforting winter concoction has a wonderful blend of vegetables with the beans. One of my father's soup tricks was to add a solid chunk of a really good quality Parmesan cheese and let it slowly disappear as the soup simmered its other flavors together. Try it!

---

1 cup dried great northern beans, washed and picked over

water to cover beans

1 tablespoon minced garlic

½ teaspoon dried thyme (or 1 teaspoon fresh thyme)

½ teaspoon dried rosemary (or 1 teaspoon fresh rosemary)

½ teaspoon kosher salt

2 bay leaves

4 tablespoons olive oil

3 carrots, cut into ½-inch pieces

2 onions, chopped

2 celery ribs, cut into ½-inch pieces

2 teaspoons minced garlic

salt and black pepper to taste

1 medium butternut squash, peeled, seeded, and cut into 1-inch chunks

½ pound green beans, trimmed and cut into ½-inch pieces

4 cups shredded green cabbage

6 cups chicken broth (or vegetable broth)

1 quart water

Parmesan cheese (optional)

2 zucchini, quartered and sliced

½ head cauliflower, cut into florets

2 cups small broccoli florets

1 28-ounce can whole tomatoes in juice, drained and chopped

---

## The Beans

In a large Dutch oven, place beans and enough cold water to cover them by 1 inch. Bring to a boil, remove from heat, cover, and let stand for 1 hour. Drain the beans, rinse, and return to the pot; cover with 2 inches of cold water. Add the garlic, thyme, rosemary, salt, and bay leaves and bring to a boil. Reduce heat and simmer covered for 30 minutes. Drain the beans and set aside.

## The Rest of the Soup

Heat 2 tablespoons of the olive oil in the Dutch oven. Add carrots, onions, celery, and garlic; salt and pepper to taste. Cook for about 8 minutes over medium-high heat until the vegetables are softened.

Add the drained beans, squash, green beans, cabbage, broth, and water. This would be a good time to add that hunk of Parmesan cheese I mentioned earlier. Bring to a boil and then simmer for 30 minutes.

Stir in the zucchini, cauliflower, and broccoli. Continue simmering partially covered for about 20 more minutes or until the vegetables are tender. Add the chopped tomatoes and cook 10 more minutes.

Remove approximately 2 cups of the soup to a blender and purée; return to pot to thicken the soup.

I cannot think of a more soul-warming dish for a cold winter night than this pot full of health, warmth, and protein.

*Per serving:* calories 359, calories from fat 78, total fat 9 g, cholesterol 0 mg, carbohydrates 54 g, fiber 15 g, protein 20 g

# WHITE BEAN AND AVOCADO GAZPACHO

6 SERVINGS

Gazpacho is a cold Spanish soup made from fresh tomatoes. By adding the protein of beans to the various other fresh vegetables that combine to create this wonderfully refreshing lunch or dinner first course, we have rounded out the nutrition factor enormously. Keep in mind that you can ensure the success of your gazpacho by using the freshest produce possible.

1 46-ounce can tomato juice

1 clove garlic, minced

½ onion, minced

3 cups fresh tomatoes, chopped

½ cup diced green bell pepper

½ cup diced red sweet pepper

1 cucumber, peeled, seeded, and chopped

1 can great northern beans, drained and rinsed

2 cups cooked white corn, preferably cut straight from the cob

½ cup fresh cilantro, finely chopped

½ cup fresh parsley, chopped

¼ cup balsamic vinegar

¼ cup green onion, chopped (both white and green parts)

1 tablespoon sugar

1 tablespoon ground cumin

¼ cup olive oil

1 jalapeño, minced, to taste

Tabasco to taste

juice of ½ fresh lemon

juice of 1 fresh lime

kosher salt to taste

ground pepper to taste

2 avocados, peeled, chopped, and sprinkled with fresh lime juice

In a large saucepan, bring the tomato juice to just the beginning of a boil. Remove from heat and add all the ingredients, except the avocado. Cool completely and stir in the avocado. Refrigerate for at least 4 hours to let the flavors blend and richen. Croutons and an extra sprinkle of cilantro round out the presentation.

Serve very cold on a hot summer day with a crisp white wine and a fresh, hot baguette.

*Per serving:* calories 670, calories from fat 181, total fat 21 g, cholesterol 0 mg, carbohydrates 119 g, fiber 17 g, protein 24 g

# ZUPPA DI FAGIOLI ALLA TOSCANA
## (Italian Bean Soup) 6 TO 8 SERVINGS

The Italian province of Tuscany lies northwest of Rome. One of the most-loved foods of Tuscans is the lowly bean, so if you see the term "alla Toscana," very likely there are beans in the dish. So follows an "alla Toscana," since no bean cookbook would be complete without at least one such version. This came from my mother, Josephine. She was a chef extraordinaire in her day. As this soup proves, somehow the time invested in preparing a recipe is always reflected in the taste. If nothing else, this soup will make a "mangia fagioli" (bean eater) out of you.

2 cups dried navy or great northern beans, washed and picked over

2 quarts water

2 small bay leaves

⅓ cup olive oil

½ cup finely diced onion

3 cloves garlic, minced

¼ cup chopped fresh parsley

salt and freshly ground black pepper to taste

Parmesan cheese to taste

Cover the washed beans with water. Bring to a boil and remove from the heat. Let stand for at least 1 hour. Drain well.

Add the water and bay leaves. Bring to a boil; reduce heat and simmer for 3 hours.

With a slotted spoon, remove about one-half of the beans. Place in a food processor and process until chopped and almost smooth. Return the puréed beans to the soup.

In a skillet, heat the olive oil and sauté the onions until soft and done, but not brown.

Add the garlic and sauté for 1 to 2 minutes. Add this to the soup.

Stir in parsley and cook for about 10 minutes over low heat.

Add salt and pepper to taste.

Serve in big, deep soup bowls with extra parsley and Parmesan cheese sprinkled liberally over the top. Add a salad, hard crusty Italian bread, and a robust red wine.

*Per serving:* calories 506, calories from fat 89, total fat 10 g, cholesterol 0, carbohydrates 77 g, fiber 19 g, protein 30 g

# TWO PASTA AND BEAN SOUP

6 SERVINGS

This thick, comfy soup is great for a weekday meal or to have in the freezer in case someone gets a cold. (Instant cure!) Splurge a little on the olive oil that goes into this soup. The flavor of a high-quality, fruity extra virgin olive oil is very important to this dish.

1 tablespoon extra virgin olive oil

1 cup chopped celery

3 carrots, chopped

1 cup chopped onion

1 tablespoon minced garlic

1 tablespoon dried parsley

½ teaspoon dried rosemary

4 cups chicken broth (or vegetable broth)

2 cups water

8 ounces rotini pasta

5 plum tomatoes, chopped

1 cup pastina pasta

1 15.5-ounce can cannellini beans, drained and rinsed

grated Asiago or Parmesan cheese to taste

In a large soup pot, heat oil over medium heat. Add celery, carrots, onion, garlic, parsley, and rosemary. Sauté, stirring, until vegetables are soft, about 4 to 5 minutes.

Add the broth and water to the vegetables and bring to a boil. Add the rotini pasta and cook for 6 minutes.

Add the tomatoes, pastina, and beans and cook until soup is thickened, about 7 to 8 more minutes.

Have the grated cheese available for sprinkling on top of each serving, to taste.

*Per serving:* calories 219, calories from fat 35, total fat 4 g, cholesterol 0 mg, carbohydrates 37 g, fiber 3 g, protein 9 g

# BARBECUE BEANS

6 TO 8 SERVINGS

Absolutely great at a summer barbeque. This has the taste of a dish that, prior to this recipe, only grandmothers and great aunts brought to family picnics.

1–2 tablespoons olive oil

3 onions, chopped

2 tablespoons minced garlic

2 cups navy beans, picked over, rinsed, and soaked 8–12 hours in water to cover

1 teaspoon dried rosemary leaves

½ teaspoon dried thyme

3 tablespoons chili powder

3 carrots, sliced

water to cover beans

⅓ cup molasses

3 tablespoons prepared, coarse-grained mustard

1½ tablespoons apple cider vinegar

sea salt to taste

Drain and rinse the beans well.

Heat oil in a large Dutch oven and sauté onions and garlic, stirring, until the onions are golden, about 2 to 3 minutes. Add the drained beans, rosemary, thyme, chili powder, carrots, and enough water to just cover the mixture.

Bring to a boil; reduce heat and simmer on low, partially covered, for 1½ to 2 hours, until beans are tender.

Stir in the molasses, mustard, cider vinegar, and salt. Simmer, covered, another 15 minutes until the final flavors blend.

HINT: This is best the next day. The flavors deepen, the liquid thickens, and it is just all around better if you prepare this the day before the picnic and reheat the next day.

*Per serving:* calories 140, calories from fat 9, total fat 1 g, cholesterol 0 mg, carbohydrates 29 g, fiber 5 g, protein 5 g

# "BOSTON BAKED BEANS"

8 SERVINGS

One cannot own a bean book that does not contain this recipe. This is a meatless version of the famous New England dish. Once the beans are finished soaking, it's a cinch to put together. And the 8-hour cooking time will give you all kinds of time to get that "stuff" done in the house you've been putting off.

---

1 pound dry great northern beans

2 medium onions, chopped

2 teaspoons apple cider vinegar

2 teaspoons prepared mustard

1 teaspoon sea salt

⅓ cup brown sugar

⅓ cup molasses

1 teaspoon ground ginger

¾ cup tomato juice

¼ cup ketchup

¼ cup melted shortening

---

Preheat oven to a temperature no hotter than 250° F.

Soak the beans in 10 cups of water overnight. After the beans have soaked, drain and rinse well. Place the beans in a large oven casserole or "bean pot." Add the chopped onion to the pot.

In a separate bowl, mix the vinegar, mustard, salt, brown sugar, molasses, ginger, tomato juice, and ketchup.

Pour the vinegar mixture over the beans and onion in the pot.

Pour the shortening over all.

Cook in an oven no hotter than 250° F for 7 to 8 hours.

*Per serving:* calories 301, calories from fat 62, total fat 7 g, cholesterol 0 mg, carbohydrates 51 g, fiber 10 g, protein 11g

# ORIENTAL BEANS

6 SERVINGS

I guess you would call this "stir-fry" beans. The flavors and technique definitely apply.

---

2 tablespoons peanut oil

1 large onion, diced in large pieces

1 tablespoon minced garlic

2 cups broccoli florets

1 tablespoon black bean sauce

2 tablespoons lemon juice

2 tablespoons tamari soy sauce

pinch of red pepper flakes

2 15-ounce cans great northern beans, drained and rinsed

1 cup chicken broth (or vegetable broth)

---

Heat the peanut oil in a large skillet or wok. Stir-fry the onions, garlic, and broccoli for about 2 minutes, stirring constantly.

Add the black bean sauce, lemon juice, tamari, and red pepper flakes, stirring to mix well.

Add the beans and broth. Lower heat and simmer for 20 minutes.

Serve over a nice brown rice. A completely different side dish for just about any type of meal.

*Per serving:* calories 481, calories from fat 55, total fat 6 g, cholesterol 0 mg, carbohydrates 81 g, fiber 25 g, protein 29 g

# VEGETABLE AND WHITE BEAN ROAST

4 TO 6 SERVINGS

This has it all. Serving this dish over a brown basmati rice rounds out both the flavor and the protein.

1 medium eggplant, cubed

1 yellow pepper, diced

1 medium red onion, chopped

1 green pepper, chopped

1 large zucchini squash, cubed

2 cups cannellini beans, cooked, rinsed, and drained

1 tablespoon minced garlic

fresh ground black pepper to taste

3 tablespoons Braggs Amino Acids or light soy sauce

1 tablespoon sesame seeds

3 tablespoons olive oil

Preheat oven to 350° F.

Place vegetables and beans in a roasting pan. Add the garlic, black pepper, Braggs Amino Acids, sesame seeds, and olive oil and stir to coat thoroughly.

Cover with aluminum foil and bake for 45 minutes.

*Per serving:* calories 323, calories from fat 72, total fat 8 g, cholesterol 0 mg, carbohydrates 48 g, fiber 12 g, protein 18 g

# BARBUNYALI PLAKI

6 TO 8 SERVINGS

Hmm.... You don't need to be able to pronounce the name to enjoy this version of a popular Turkish dish. Just be sure to serve it chilled.

4–5 tablespoons olive oil

2 onions, diced

2 tablespoons minced garlic

¼ cup finely chopped fresh parsley (plus extra 6–8 sprigs for garnish)

2 carrots, finely chopped

8 plum tomatoes, diced

2 15-ounce cans navy beans, rinsed and drained

water to cover mixture

6–8 lemon wedges

In a soup pot, heat oil and sauté onion, garlic, parsley, and carrots. When the onions become soft, add tomatoes and beans, stirring to mix. Add just enough water to barely cover the bean mixture. Bring to a simmer and cook for 20 minutes.

Chill and serve topped with a sprig of fresh parsley and lemon wedges.

*Per serving:* calories 297, calories from fat 106, total fat 12 g, cholesterol 0 mg, carbohydrates 38 g, fiber 9 g, protein 11 g

# Main Dishes

. . . . . . . . . . . . . . . . . . . . . . . . . . . . . . . . .

## PASTA WITH ASPARAGUS, BUTTER BEANS, AND CARAMELIZED ONIONS 4 SERVINGS

You might make this dish because it's vegetarian and packed with protein, plant nutrients, and a goodly portion of carbohydrates. But the best reason of all is that it's absolutely delicious.

---

8 ounces fusilli pasta

1 bunch young asparagus (woody stem ends snapped off)

2 tablespoons extra virgin olive oil

2 red onions, thinly sliced

1 teaspoon sugar

2 cloves garlic, chopped

½ cup chicken broth (or vegetable broth)

½ cup white wine

1 15.5-ounce can butter beans, drained and rinsed

2 large tomatoes, diced

pinch of kosher salt

¾ cup freshly grated Parmesan cheese

freshly ground black pepper to taste

---

Cook the fusilli in lightly salted boiling water for 11 minutes. Add the asparagus and cook for another 3 minutes. Drain into a colander.

While pasta is cooking, heat the oil in a large skillet. Add the onions and sugar and cook, stirring for about 10 minutes or until the onions are browned. Add the garlic, broth, and wine. Bring the mixture to a boil and simmer for 5 minutes. Add butter beans, tomatoes, and a pinch of kosher salt and toss the mixture with the pasta and asparagus. Top each serving with the Parmesan cheese and freshly ground black pepper.

Enjoy with a mesclun salad with all the trimmings!

The pasta is always interchangeable, so don't hesitate to use your own favorite type.

*Per serving:* calories 418, calories from fat 122, total fat 14 g, cholesterol 15 mg, carbohydrates 52 g, fiber 11 g, protein 17 g

# WHITE BEANS NIÇOISES

6 SERVINGS

With the addition of much more protein and fiber, this is a slightly different version of an all-time summer favorite.

---

2 6-ounce cans chunk white tuna in water, drained

2 15.5-ounce cans cannellini beans, drained and rinsed

½ cup large pitted black olives, sliced

3 tablespoons extra virgin olive oil

2 tablespoons balsamic vinegar

3 tablespoons chopped fresh parsley

6 curly green lettuce leaves

4 hard boiled eggs, cut into 4 wedges each

½ red onion, thinly sliced

kosher salt and freshly ground black pepper to taste

---

Break up the tuna with a fork and toss with the beans, olives, olive oil, vinegar, and parsley.

Arrange on lettuce leaves. Place 4 wedges of the hard boiled egg around each plate and place several slices of the red onion on top of all. Drizzle a small amount of extra virgin olive oil over each serving. Add salt and pepper to taste.

*Per serving:* calories 655, calories from fat 131, total fat 15 g, cholesterol 185 mg, carbohydrates 83 g, fiber 21 g, protein 50 g

# FLORENTINE BEANS AND PASTA

8 SERVINGS

The spinach makes it a Florentine, the great flavor combination makes it delicious!

---

1 16-ounce box spiral pasta

2 tablespoons minced garlic

2 tablespoons olive oil

2 cups chicken broth (or vegetable broth)

2 10-ounce packages frozen chopped spinach

2 15-ounce cans white beans, drained and rinsed

crushed red pepper flakes

grated Parmesan cheese to taste

---

In a large saucepan, cook pasta according to directions and drain.

In a large skillet, sauté garlic in olive oil until garlic is very light gold. Add broth and spinach, cooking according to spinach package directions.

Stir in beans and pasta. Cook uncovered over medium-high heat until heated through.

Season with the crushed red pepper and Parmesan cheese to taste and offer crusty Italian bread to soak up this delicious broth.

*Per serving:* calories 634, calories from fat 67, total fat 8 g, cholesterol 5 mg, carbohydrates 107 g, fiber 19 g, protein 37 g

# TORTELLINI WITH ESCAROLE AND BEANS

4 SERVINGS

This very simple, nutritious dish can easily be doubled to feed a crowd on a cold Saturday afternoon.

---

1 large bunch of escarole, well-washed and coarsely chopped

2 quarts water

1 8-ounce package cheese tortellini

3 tablespoons olive oil

1 large clove garlic, thinly sliced

1 small onion, chopped

1 15-ounce can cannellini beans, drained and rinsed

½ cup chicken broth (or vegetable broth)

---

In a large saucepan, cook the escarole in boiling water, covered, for 1 minute. Drain.

Refill the same saucepan with about 2 quarts water and bring to a boil. Drop in the tortellini, bring back to a boil, and cook for 3 minutes. Drain.

In a large skillet, heat olive oil, add garlic and onion, and cook over low heat for about 2 minutes.

Add the escarole, beans, broth, and cooked tortellini; cover and simmer over low heat for about 8 minutes.

Any leftovers turn into the perfect comfort food snack for a late-night munch.

*Per serving:* calories 581, calories from fat 126, total fat 14 g, cholesterol 34 mg, carbohydrates 83 g, fiber 18 g, protein 33 g

# PORTOBELLO, BEAN, AND CHEESE OPEN-FACE SANDWICHES

4 SERVINGS

It is absolutely true that a grilled portobello mushroom tastes like steak. This open-face creation will fill your stomach and delight your senses with the richness of all it's flavors. It seems like a lot of steps, but it actually goes together very easily.

## Grilled Mushrooms

3 tablespoons olive oil

1 tablespoon balsamic vinegar

1 teaspoon minced garlic

1 tablespoon minced fresh parsley

salt and pepper to taste

½ teaspoon sugar

4 large portobello mushroom caps, stems removed

Whisk together olive oil, vinegar, garlic, parsley, salt, pepper, and sugar. Brush the marinade over both sides of the mushroom caps and let sit for one hour, turning once.

Grill mushrooms over a hot flame until just soft and starting to shrink (about 3 minutes per side).

## Bean Mixture

1 15-ounce can great northern beans, drained and rinsed

1 tablespoon fresh chopped parsley

1 tablespoon fresh lemon juice

salt and pepper to taste

2 tablespoons olive oil

2 cloves garlic, thinly sliced

Using a potato masher, mash together the beans, parsley, lemon juice, salt, and pepper.

In a large skillet, heat oil and sliced garlic. Add the mashed bean mixture and sauté until heated through.

## Spinach

1 tablespoon olive oil

1 bag prewashed baby spinach leaves

Preheat oven to 450° F.

Heat the oil in a large skillet over medium-high heat and add the spinach. Stir about 2 to 3 minutes or until the spinach is wilted and soft.

Brush olive oil on one side of 4 1-inch thick slices of Italian bread. Place on a cookie sheet and bake until lightly toasted on the oiled side.

Divide the bean mixture into 4 parts and spread onto the untoasted side of the bread slices. Top each with ¼ of the wilted spinach and 1 portobello mushroom. Add one slice of mozzarella cheese and place under a broiler until the cheese is just bubbling.

Serve with some fresh sliced tomatoes with basil and olive oil on the side and hope your appetite holds out to accommodate all this wonderfulness.

*For topping, per serving:* calories 486, calories from fat 140, total fat 16 g, cholesterol 16 mg, carbohydrates 60 g, fiber 20 g, protein 29 g

# FROM THE LAND OF MILK AND HONEY

8 SERVINGS

Yes, beans and honey. This casserole is so simple, clean, and different, I imagine it is indeed a recipe from that other time and place.

2 cups dry small white beans

½ teaspoon ground ginger

1 cup finely chopped onions

½ cup sour cream

1½ teaspoons salt

pinch of freshly ground black pepper

3 tablespoons honey

1 cup boiling water

Preheat oven to 350° F.

Soak beans in warm water for 2 hours. Drain the water, add the same amount of fresh water, and bring to a boil. Reduce heat, add the ginger, and simmer for 1 hour. If you need to add more water to keep the beans covered, do so. Drain and turn beans into a greased casserole. Stir in the onions, sour cream, salt, pepper, honey, and boiling water. Cover and bake for 2 hours.

When you serve this as a side or as a dinner, top with some fresh chopped parsley. As a dinner, this works well with wild rice and a baked acorn squash. Healthy and timeless in its taste.

*Per serving:* calories 211, calories from fat 22, total fat 3g, cholesterol 6 mg, carbohydrates 38 g, fiber 12 g, protein 11 g

# CURRIED BEAN SANDWICH SPREAD

FILLING FOR 4 SANDWICHES

Have fun putting this sandwich together. Of course, I have my own suggestions, but definitely have at it and create! One possibility is slicing an 8-inch section of a whole grain baguette lengthwise and spreading ½ cup of this spread in the middle. Layer very thin slices of a granny smith apple over the spread, and sprinkle with thinly sliced scallions and curly lettuce. Any of the classic curry condiments will go nicely on any sandwich you invent.

---

¾ cup water

1 onion, finely chopped

1 cup diced celery

1 green bell pepper, diced

½ cup thinly sliced carrots

2 cloves garlic, minced

3 teaspoons curry powder

½ teaspoon ground cumin

1 tablespoon soy sauce

3 cups cooked great northern beans

---

Place water, onion, celery, green pepper, carrot, and garlic in a saucepan. Cook over medium-high heat, stirring occasionally, for 15 minutes

Stir in the curry powder, cumin, and soy sauce and mix well. Remove from heat. Add the beans and mix well again.

Place the mixture into a food processor or blender and process briefly until chopped but not puréed.

Chill well.

*Filling, per serving:* calories 112, calories from fat 12, total fat 1 g, cholesterol 0 mg, carbohydrates 99 g, fiber 25 g, protein 37 g

# PASTA E FAGIOLI (Pasta and Beans)

4 SERVINGS

This and the following recipe, "Escarole and Fagioli," are home. They are Friday evenings in winter after school and homework. They are the smell of garlic and sauce and everything that makes coming home smell like coming home. I'm not sure whose recipes these are—my mother's or my father's—but they each made them and you could not tell one from the other. Once again, getting amounts for a recipe from mothers, grandmothers, etc., is a challenge, as they tend to use the space in the cup of their hand as a measure.

---

1 stalk celery, thinly sliced

1 small onion, diced

3 tablespoons olive oil

2–3 cloves of garlic, thinly sliced

1 32-ounce can crushed tomatoes

2–3 tablespoons tomato paste

1 tablespoon chopped fresh parsley
   (or 1½ teaspoon dried)

1 tablespoon chopped fresh basil (or
   1½ teaspoon dried)

1 teaspoon dried oregano

salt and pepper to taste

1 cup tubettini pasta

1 15-ounce can cannellini beans

Parmesan or Romano cheese to taste

---

In a 3-quart saucepan, sauté celery and onion in oil until onion is transparent. Add garlic and sauté until lightly gold. Add the can of tomatoes and stir in the tomato paste, parsley, basil, and oregano. Add the salt and pepper. Cook until slightly thickened, about 15 to 20 minutes.

Cook tubettini as per directions on the box for *al dente*. Drain and add to the sauce along with the cannellini beans. Stir and continue to cook for another 10 minutes.

Top with Parmesan or Romano cheese to taste.

*Per serving:* calories 582, calories from fat 105, total fat 12 g, cholesterol 0 mg, carbohydrates 94 g, fiber 19 g, protein 30 g

# ESCAROLE E FAGIOLI (Greens and Beans)

4 TO 6 SERVINGS

Greens and Beans are so simple, so basic, so peasant, and so fulfilling.

1 head escarole

4 tablespoons olive oil

3 cloves garlic, thinly sliced

salt and pepper to taste

½ cup fresh chopped parsley

1 cup chicken broth (or water)

2 15-ounce cans cannellini beans, drained and rinsed

crushed red pepper flakes to taste

Halve the escarole heads, cutting off the bottoms. Wash extremely well to remove all dirt and drain well.

Sauté the garlic in the olive oil until lightly golden. Set aside to cool for a few minutes before adding escarole, salt, pepper, parsley, and broth. Cook for 5 minutes on high heat, stirring constantly. Lower heat and simmer for about 25 minutes. Stir in beans and cook until beans are hot.

Add those red pepper flakes to taste on each individual serving.

This can be prepared with Savoy cabbage or almost any green. And don't forget the Italian bread—you gotta have it with this.

*Per serving:* calories 545, calories from fat 93, total fat 11 g, cholesterol 0 mg, carbohydrates 83 g, fiber 22 g, protein 33 g

# PASTA FAGIOLE II—ALLA PETRINA

6 SERVINGS

Suzie Gance Rommel's variation on the more traditional Pasta Fagiole has a richer taste and a combination of flavors so different from the Pasta Fagiole of my Friday dinner memories. Suz has once again managed to create the extraordinary out of the ordinary in food just as she does with life. Thank you, Suzie!

2 tablespoons extra virgin olive oil, plus extra for drizzling later

1 medium onion, chopped

1 celery rib, chopped

1 medium fennel bulb, trimmed and cut into strips ¼-inch wide

4 cloves garlic, pressed through a garlic press

1 teaspoon dried oregano

½ teaspoon fennel seed

¼ teaspoon red pepper flakes

2 teaspoons orange zest

6 anchovies, mashed (or 1 tablespoon anchovy paste)

1 28-ounce can diced tomatoes, with liquid

1 piece of Parmesan cheese rind, about 3 x 4 inches in size

2 cans canellini beans, drained and rinsed

3½ cups chicken broth (or vegetable broth)

2 cups water

½ pound orzo pasta

freshly ground black pepper to taste

extra Parmesan for topping

In a large saucepan, heat olive oil and sauté onion, celery, and fennel over medium heat until the onion is translucent.

Add pressed garlic, oregano, fennel seed, and red pepper. Add orange zest and anchovy, stirring constantly for 1 minute. Stir in the diced tomatoes with liquid and the piece of Parmesan rind. Bring to a boil; reduce heat and simmer for 10 minutes.

Add the cannellini beans, chicken broth, and water. Bring back to a boil and add the orzo pasta. Simmer until the orzo is tender.

Find the cheese rind and remove. Serve this in big, wonderful soup bowls with the olive oil available for drizzling and extra Parmesan for topping on individual servings.

*Per serving:* calories 676, calories from fat 64, total fat 7 g, cholesterol 0 mg, carbohydrates 116 g, fiber 22 g, protein 40 g

# WHITE BEAN-STUFFED ACORN SQUASH

4 SERVINGS

This colorful, high-fiber treat would make a great dinner for a crisp autumn evening and a perfect addition to any Thanksgiving table.

---

2 tablespoons olive oil

2 large onions, diced

1 large carrot, diced

1 tablespoon minced garlic

1 15.5-ounce can cannellini beans, drained and rinsed

¾ cup chicken broth (or vegetable broth)

sea salt and fresh ground black pepper to taste

3 teaspoons chopped fresh basil (divided use)

2 small acorn squashes

1 large tomato, chopped

grated Parmesan cheese

---

In a medium-size skillet, heat oil over medium-high heat. Add onions, carrots, and garlic. Cook 15 minutes or until vegetables are tender and onion is golden, stirring occasionally. Add beans, broth, salt, pepper, and 2 teaspoons of the basil. Bring to a boil. Cover skillet and keep warm on low heat.

Cut each squash in half lengthwise and remove seeds. Place squash halves in a microwave-safe baking dish. Cover and cook in the microwave oven on high for 6 to 8 minutes or until squash is tender. (Or, cook squash in a 375° F oven for approximately 35 to 45 minutes or until squash is fork-tender.)

Place squash halves on a platter. Fill each half with ¼ of the bean mixture. Sprinkle with chopped tomato and remaining chopped basil. Top with a sprinkling of Parmesan cheese and garnish with a beautiful sprig of fresh and fragrant basil.

This colorful, high-fiber treat would fit in well on a Thanksgiving table or served as a dinner for a crisp fall night.

*Per serving:* calories 392, calories from fat 63, total fat 8 g, cholesterol 0 mg, carbohydrates 83 g, fiber 22 g, protein 27 g

# PASTA WITH BEANS, BASIL, AND CORN

6 SERVINGS

This should be made in the summer only. The flavors of the fresh basil and fresh-picked corn cannot be duplicated with the winter replacements you find in the grocery stores.

---

6 ears fresh corn

12 ounces orecchiette pasta (little hats)

1 15-ounce can great northern beans, drained and rinsed

2 cups fresh basil (extra for garnish)

sea salt to taste

4 tablespoons extra virgin olive oil

3 tablespoons balsamic vinegar

1 red pepper, diced

1 yellow pepper, diced

---

Cut the kernels off the uncooked cobs and set aside.

Cook the pasta according to the package instruction for *al dente*. Add the corn kernels to the pot for the last 30 seconds. Drain the pasta and corn in a colander and transfer to a large bowl.

Add the beans, basil, salt, olive oil, vinegar, and peppers and gently toss until blended.

This can be served warm or at room temperature. Sprinkle with additional fresh chopped basil for an extra color and flavor splash.

*Per serving:* calories 322, calories from fat 98, total fat 11 g, cholesterol 0 mg, carbohydrates 50 g, fiber 9 g, protein 12 g

# GNOCCHI

6 SERVINGS

If you already know what these are, then you know the correct pronunciation.* If you don't, pronounce it the way it looks—for the entertainment of those of us who know! Gnocchi are traditionally made with potatoes or ricotta cheese, but this is a great version that cuts down on the carbs and ups the protein and fiber of this classic Italian dish.

---

1 15.5-ounce can cannellini beans, drained and rinsed

3 tablespoons water

1 cup ricotta cheese

1 egg

¾ cup chopped frozen spinach, thawed and drained

2 cups flour

pinch of salt

---

In a food processor or blender, purée the beans with 3 tablespoons water until smooth and creamy.

Mix the beans, ricotta cheese, egg, and spinach.

Sift the flour and salt. Make a well in the center. Add the bean mixture and work until you form a ball. Let rest for 10 minutes.

Break off one piece of dough at a time and roll into a thick, cordlike rope, about ¾ inch in diameter. (You may need flour on your hands and a sprinkling on a board to roll the dough.) Cut this cord into smaller pieces of about ¾ inch in length. Then roll each of these pieces into a small bullet-shaped pasta, with an indentation in its center.

Fill a large pot ¾ full of water and bring to a boil. Gently add gnocchi. After 2 to 3 minutes, gently stir. Gnocchi are usually done when they float to the top, but test after 5 minutes. They should be the consistency of a thick macaroni, and some prefer them *al dente*.

Drain and mix with your favorite tomato sauce. Top with a grated Parmesan and Romano cheese blend.

For "gnocchi Parmigiana," place the cooked gnocchi into a casserole and top with sauce, ½ cup of the Parmesan and Romano blend, and 1 cup of grated mozzarella cheese. Place into a preheated 450° F oven for 4 to 5 minutes or until cheese is melted and bubbling.

*Say "NYOE-kee"

*Per serving:* calories 451, calories from fat 46, total fat 5 g, cholesterol 54 mg, carbohydrates 75 g, fiber 12 g, protein 26 g

# PASTA PUTTANESCA WITH CANNELLINI BEANS

6 SERVINGS

Even if you hate anchovies, you will never realize their presence in this dish. The dissipated flavor adds a subtle richness and depth to this quick dinner that would be missed if you gave in to your misgivings. This Italian dish is a version of a pasta named for a group of women practicing the oldest profession in the world. Since they didn't have much time for cooking, this was easily and quickly put together and filled the stomachs of their families in a nourishing way.

1 tablespoon extra virgin olive oil

1 large onion, chopped

4 cloves garlic, minced

3 anchovies, minced

2 tablespoons red wine vinegar

2 teaspoons dried basil (or 4 teaspoons chopped fresh basil)

1 tablespoon tomato paste

1 28-ounce can whole plum tomatoes

½ cup pitted green olives, chopped

1 tablespoon capers

1 15-ounce can cannellini beans, drained and rinsed

red pepper flakes to taste

12 ounces fettuccini

Heat oil in a large skillet or saucepan over medium-high heat. Add onion and garlic and cook 3 to 4 minutes or until soft, stirring frequently. Add anchovies and sauté about 2 minutes longer.

Add vinegar, basil, tomato paste, tomatoes, olives, and capers, bringing mixture to a boil. Reduce heat and simmer for 15 minutes. Add beans and pepper flakes and cook 4 minutes longer.

Cook fettuccini in a large pot of salted water; drain and rinse.

Put fettuccini on a large platter and top with the Puttanesca sauce.

Chianti, an antipasto platter, crisp Italian bread—oh my!

*Per serving:* calories 500, calories from fat 42, total fat 5 g, cholesterol 0 mg, carbohydrates 92 g, fiber 14 g, protein 25 g

# TOMATO AND WHITE BEAN CASSEROLE

6 SERVINGS

The red, white, and green of this dish appropriately signals the taste of Italy.

---

1½ cups Italian seasoned breadcrumbs

2 tablespoons extra virgin olive oil (divided use)

2 medium onions, minced

2 cloves garlic, minced

1 28-ounce can whole tomatoes, chopped (reserve juice)

1 teaspoon minced fresh thyme leaves

2 teaspoons finely chopped fresh basil

2 15-ounce cans cannellini beans, drained and rinsed

1 bunch fresh spinach leaves, washed well

salt and fresh ground pepper to taste

---

Mix bread crumbs and 1 tablespoon of the oil in a small bowl and set aside.

Heat remaining oil in a large skillet and add onions. Sauté over medium heat about 3 minutes or until onions are just soft. Add garlic and sauté until just sizzling. Add tomatoes with juice, thyme, and basil. Add beans and spinach; bring to a boil and simmer until spinach is wilted and mixture starts to thicken.

Season with salt and pepper.

Transfer mixture to an 8-inch square baking dish and sprinkle breadcrumb mixture evenly over all. Place under broiler until the crumbs are golden brown. Avoid burning them.

Let cool for 2 to 3 minutes before serving.

*Per serving:* calories 512, calories from fat 52, total fat 6 g, cholesterol 0 mg, carbohydrates 86 g, fiber 22 g, protein 33 g

# Desserts

. . . . . . . . . . . . . . . . . . . . . . . . . . . . . . .

## COCONUT CUSTARD

6 SERVINGS

This is another creation by Eugenio Concepción Sepúlveda of Boqueron, Puerto Rico. This extraordinarily light dessert or breakfast custard is sugar free, low fat, high protein, and exceptionally tasty.

1 15.5-ounce can cannellini beans, drained and rinsed

1 8-ounce package light cream cheese

6 small packages Splenda

1 can light coconut milk

1 pint Egg Beaters (or any egg substitute equivalent to 4 eggs)

Preheat oven to 350° F.

Blend the first four ingredients in a food processor until smooth. Add Egg Beaters ¼ cup at a time, blending between each addition.

Pour the custard into an 8-inch cake dish. Place the dish in a flat pan that has about 1 inch of water in it. Bake for 45 to 60 minutes until a knife inserted in the center of the custard comes out clean.

Let cool for 15 minutes and invert on a platter. Chill in refrigerator for at least an hour. This looks quite beautiful when served with a dollop of whipped cream and a sprinkling of fresh raspberries. Never hesitate to add a splash of green when available, i.e., a sprig of mint.

*Per serving:* calories 274, calories from fat 35, total fat 5 g, cholesterol 0 mg, carbohydrates 43 g, fiber 10 g, protein 16 g

# CHOCOLATE COVERED "MARZIPAN"

ABOUT 20 MARZIPAN BALLS

This recipe takes marzipan, a classic almond-flavored holiday candy, from just another sugary treat to a nutritious yet sweet little morsel that you'll be hard put to tell from the original.

## Marzipan

3½ ounces pure almond paste (½ tube Odense almond paste)

1 15.5-ounce can great northern beans, drained and rinsed

2 tablespoons almond extract

½ cup Splenda or sugar

1 cup finely ground almonds (a food processor works well)

Process almond paste in food processor until crumbly; remove and place in medium-size bowl.

Place the beans and almond extract in a food processor and purée until very smooth. Add in sweetener and mix well.

Turn the bean mixture into the bowl with the almond paste and add the ground almonds. Stir to mix well.

Another flavor option would be to stir 1 cup of coconut into the bean mixture.

## Chocolate Coating

6 ounces semisweet baking chocolate bars broken into small pieces

½ stick sweet butter

Place the chocolate and butter in a small microwave-safe dish and heat on high for 10- to 20-second intervals, stirring until smooth and melted.

Form the dough into walnut-size balls and dip each ball into the melted chocolate while it's still warm. Place each ball carefully on a cookie sheet covered with waxed paper, taking care that they don't touch each other. Place in the refrigerator and chill for at least 1 hour.

I dare you to serve these on a Christmas buffet or on any holiday, for that matter. They will disappear.

*Per ball:* calories 155, calories from fat 83, total fat 10 g, cholesterol 6 mg, carbohydrates 15 g, fiber 3 g, protein 4 g

# OATMEAL CHOCOLATE CHIP COOKIES

ABOUT 36 COOKIES

This is all they need to be called. No mention of beans is necessary! We all know it takes a bit of scheming for any parent to get a child to eat right, and this recipe is devious. The extra fiber, protein, calcium, and iron that these cookies contain outweighs any guilt you may feel about failing to mention the secret ingredient.

1 15.5-ounce can great northern beans, drained and rinsed

2 tablespoons water

1 tablespoon plus 2 teaspoons vanilla (divided use)

1¾ cups flour

¾ teaspoon baking soda

¾ teaspoon baking powder

2 sticks butter

1½ cups brown sugar or Splenda

2 large eggs

3½ cups old-fashioned rolled oats

1 6-ounce bag chocolate chips

Preheat oven to 350° F.

Place beans, water, and 1 tablespoon of vanilla into a food processor and process until smooth.

In a large bowl, whisk together flour, baking soda, and baking powder.

In a separate bowl, cream together the butter and brown sugar. Add eggs and vanilla and blend until creamy. Mix in the bean mixture.

Add the butter and bean mixture to the flour and stir until well mixed. Add the oatmeal and chocolate chips.

Drop the dough by heaping tablespoonfuls onto a greased cookie sheet about 2 inches apart.

Bake for 6 to 9 minutes or until light golden brown.

*Per cookie:* calories 164, calories from fat 63, total fat 7 g, cholesterol 28 mg, carbohydrates 23 g, fiber 1 g, protein 3 g.

# PUMPKIN ALMOND OAT MUFFINS

12 MUFFINS

This is for Chris and Annie. Chris once accused Annie of trying to create the perfect food in the shape of a muffin. And it's true—Annie would make incredible muffins with every possible combination of ingredients. But, beans, Annie, beans! Beans were the missing link to nutritional perfection in your creations.

---

1 15-ounce can great northern beans, drained and rinsed

2 tablespoons water

1 15-ounce can pumpkin

½ cup vegetable or canola oil

1½ cups brown sugar or Splenda

2 large eggs

1 cup buttermilk

1 tablespoon almond extract

2 cups flour

2 teaspoons baking powder

2 teaspoons baking soda

pinch of salt

2 teaspoons cinnamon

1½ cups old fashioned rolled oats

1 cup sliced almonds

---

Preheat oven to 350° F.

Grease a standard 12-muffin pan or line with paper cups.

Purée the beans and 2 tablespoons of water in a food processor or blender until smooth.

In a medium bowl, mix together the beans and the canned pumpkin.

In a larger bowl, beat the oil and sugar, adding the eggs one at a time, beating between additions. Whisk in buttermilk and almond extract. Add the pumpkin and bean mixture.

In a separate bowl, whisk together the flour, baking powder, baking soda, salt, and cinnamon.

Add the flour mixture to the wet mixture and stir only until the flour mix is moistened. Fold in oats and almonds.

Divide the batter among the muffin cups. Bake for 20 to 22 minutes or until a toothpick inserted in the muffins comes out clean. Let cool for several minutes before removing from pan.

*Per muffin:* calories 443, calories from fat 153, total fat 8 g, cholesterol 44 mg, carbohydrates 63 g, fiber 6 g, protein 11 g

# WHITE BEAN AND BANANA BREAKFAST FRITTERS

6 SERVINGS

This is a way to begin your day with a delicious, protein and fiber-packed blast. Again, using canned beans makes this a quick and easy put-together to send yourself or your loved ones out into the new day with a nutritious push.

---

1 15.5-ounce can cannellini beans, drained, rinsed, and puréed in food processor

1 ripe banana, mashed

2 teaspoons vanilla

1 egg, lightly beaten

¼ cup maple syrup

¾ cup sugar (or ¾ cup Splenda, or 3 drops stevia)

4 teaspoons cinnamon

½ teaspoon baking soda

2 teaspoons baking powder

pinch of salt

1 cup white unbleached flour

canola oil (approximately 1 inch deep in flat fry pan)

powdered sugar

---

Mix together beans and mashed banana. Add vanilla, egg, maple syrup, and sugar. Add remainder of the ingredients except the powdered sugar and stir until you have a sticky droppable batter.

Drop by generous tablespoons into hot canola oil (375° F). Brown on both sides. Remove with a slotted spoon onto a paper towel covered platter. Sprinkle with powdered sugar.

Serve warm with fruit and yogurt and off you go, not to be hungry for a long time.

For a special treat, try adding ½ cup shredded coconut or ½ cup chopped walnuts to the batter.

*Per serving:* calories 467, calories from fat 17, total fat 2 g, cholesterol 41 mg, carbohydrates 96 g, fiber 11 g, protein 19 g

# THE GREAT MAPLE WALNUT BANANA BEAN BREAD

16 SLICES

Eat this when you're happy, eat this when you're sad, eat with milk, or sit down with a good cup of coffee. Grab a piece on the run or make time in your busy day for a snack break. This is a wonderfully nutritious snack or dessert disguised as a comfort food. Add more nuts if you want or add more cinnamon. Any way you go, a warm slice of this will only make you want another.

---

1 15.5-ounce can great northern beans, drained and rinsed

3 medium-sized, very ripe bananas

¾ cup oil (canola or vegetable)

1 cup maple syrup (or 1 cup brown sugar, or 1 cup Splenda)

1 egg

2 teaspoons vanilla

2 teaspoons baking soda

2 teaspoons baking powder

pinch of salt

1 teaspoon cinnamon

2 cups flour

¾ cup chopped walnuts

---

Preheat oven to 350° F.

Mash the beans and the bananas in a medium bowl. In a larger bowl, whisk oil and maple syrup together. Beat in the egg. Add vanilla, baking soda, baking powder, salt, and cinnamon. Add the banana and bean mixture and mix well. Stir in flour and chopped walnuts and mix well.

Pour batter into 2 greased 8-inch loaf pans and bake for 35 to 45 minutes or until a toothpick inserted in the center comes out clean.

Another thought:

Add 1 cup coconut to create a more tropical taste.

*Per slice:* calories 267, calories from fat 127, total fat 15 g, cholesterol 15 mg, carbohydrates 32 g, fiber 1 g, protein 3 g

# BEAN, I MEAN, CREAM PUFFS

12 CREAM PUFFS

Whatever, these luscious creamy little morsels will melt in your mouth and it really won't matter what type of puffs they are.

## Filling

1 15.5-ounce can cannellini beans, drained and rinsed

5 tablespoons water

4 cups milk

1 cup sugar or Splenda

2 cinnamon sticks

1 tablespoon vanilla

9 egg yolks

5 tablespoons cornstarch

Purée the beans and the water in a food processor until very smooth, with no lumps of beans remaining.

Transfer the bean purée to a heavy saucepan and whisk in 3 cups of the milk. Add the vanilla and cinnamon sticks.

In a medium-size bowl, whisk the egg yolks, cornstarch, and remaining 1 cup of milk. Pour mixture through a fine strainer into the pan with the bean purée. This is to remove any small lumps of cornstarch.

Over medium heat, stir constantly with a spoon until mixture thickens. This will take about 5 to 8 minutes. You will need a little patience here. When the mixture has a thick, custard consistency, transfer to a bowl and cool completely. Place in refrigerator when cool.

## Puffs

1 cup water

½ cup butter or margarine

½ teaspoon salt

1 cup flour

4 eggs

Preheat oven to 450° F.

Measure water and butter into a saucepan and place over medium heat until mixture boils. Add the salt and flour all at once and mix until dough forms a ball and pulls away from the side of the pan. Remove from heat. Add eggs one at a time, beating well after each addition. Drop dough about the size of walnuts onto a greased baking sheet. Reduce oven to 375° F and bake 30 to 35 minutes, until golden brown and puffed up. Remove from oven and immediately slit each puff with a small knife to allow steam to escape. Cool completely. Cut off the top to each puff and reserve. Fill with the custard and replace the top.

I find it best to fill the puffs as you are about to use them. They are quite beautiful on a silver platter with a lace doily and sprinkled with a dusting of powdered sugar. One might wish to drizzle a little chocolate sauce over them also. Tumble a couple of strawberries about the platter for a dramatic contrast.

*Per 2 puffs:* calories 388, calories from fat 127, total fat 14 g, cholesterol 264 mg, carbohydrates 51 g, fiber 6 g, protein 15 g

# PIE CRUST

MAKES ONE 9" DEEP-DISH PIE CRUST

This is the perfect way to enhance the health factor of any fruit pie by adding the protein and fiber supplied by beans.

---

1 cup cooked cannellini beans, drained and rinsed

1 teaspoon baking powder

1 egg

2 tablespoons canola oil

2 teaspoons cinnamon

1 tablespoon sugar or Splenda

1 cup flour

---

Mash the cooked beans well or purée in a food processor until smooth and creamy.

Place the beans in a large bowl. Add the rest of the ingredients and blend well with a pastry blender.

Shape the dough into a ball and roll out to about a ⅛-inch thickness on a well-floured board.

Fit into a 9-inch pie plate and fill with your favorite fruit filling to bake. Use a lattice topping or double the recipe for a 2-crust pie.

This makes a very soft, easy to handle dough. If you wish to use this crust for a quiche, omit the cinnamon and sugar.

*Per serving:* calories 191, calories from fat 41, total fat 5 g, cholesterol 31 mg, carbohydrates 30 g, fiber 5 g, protein 9 g

# Garbanzo Beans

# Garbanzo Beans

## a.k.a. Chickpeas or Ceci Beans

Garbanzo beans, also known as chickpeas or ceci beans, were originally cultivated on the lands bordering Mesopotamia and the eastern Mediterranean. Their popularity gradually spread to India and some parts of East Asia, North Africa, Spain, and southern France. As the interest in ethnic cuisine increased in the United States, they rapidly gained ground here as well, and are perhaps most well known as the main ingredient in hummus, the delicious Middle Eastern spread.

The garbanzo can be found in both a reddish or black color, but the tan variety is the most common. This uniquely sphere-shaped bean, said to resemble a ram's head, almost triples in size after soaking and cooking. When cooked, the pungent flavor blends well with garlic, onions, and spice. Garbanzos can be roasted for a crunchy snack or ground into flour for baking. They're an excellent and easy way to boost protein in salads, soups, or stews.

### Nutritional values for 1 cup of cooked garbanzo beans

Calories 286   Protein 11.8 g   Carbohydrates 54.3g   Total fat 2.7 g   Fiber 11 g
Folate 160 mcg   Vitamin B6 1.1 mg   Vitamin C 9 mg   Zinc 2.54 mg

## APPETIZERS

*Heavenly Hummus*

*Chuck's Hummus*

*Garbanzo Raita*

*Chickpea Falafel with Zesty Sauce*

*Jennifer's Bean Toasts*

*Chickpea Pot Stickers*

*Crunchy Roasted Ceci Nuts*

## SALADS, SOUPS & SIDES

*Chickpea and Couscous Salad*

*Chickpea and Spring Vegetable Salad*

*Ceci Salad*

*Ceci Bean Soup*

*Pasta and Chickpea Soup*

*Creamy Sesame Garbanzo and Spinach Soup*

*Zuppa Di Romana*

*Spicy Garbanzos and Walnuts*

*Hot and Spicy Garbanzos and Cauliflower*

*Chickpea Gravy*

## MAIN DISHES

*Linguini with Chickpeas and Anchovies*

*Moussaka*

*Garbanzos, Pasta, Spinach, and Cheese*

*Pasta Aglio, Olio*

*Garbanzos Fritos*

*Farfalle with Chickpeas, Zucchini, and Tomatoes*

*Cuccia*

*Chana Masala*

*Garbanzos alla Jardinera*

*Green Garbanzo Gumbo*

*Chickpea and Eggplant Stew*

*Chickpea African Stew*

*North African Garbanzo and Fava Bean Stew*

*Chickpea Frittata*

## DESSERTS

*Coconut Walnut Chickpea Pie*

*Ciambaloni*

*Pumpkin Pie*

*Cinnamon Garbanzo Bread*

*Walnut Chocolate Chip Garbanzo Cake*

# Appetizers

## HEAVENLY HUMMUS

2 CUPS, 6 SERVINGS

Making hummus can be such an adventure. You just need a food processor or a blender and a dash of imagination. Here is a wonderful, traditional hummus, sure to please hummus lovers of all persuasions.

---

1 tablespoon sesame oil

1 small onion, chopped

1 clove garlic, minced

1 tablespoon light olive oil

1 16-ounce can garbanzo beans, drained and rinsed

2 tablespoons sesame seeds, lightly toasted

½ cup tahini (sesame butter)

¼ cup fresh lemon juice

½ teaspoon turmeric

pinch of kosher or sea salt

---

Sauté onions and garlic in sesame oil until just tender. Purée beans in a food processor, adding the onion, garlic, and remaining ingredients and blend until smooth, adding more sesame oil if too thick. Garnish with fresh parsley and extra toasted sesame seeds.

*Per serving:* calories 278, calories from fat 150, total fat 18 g, cholesterol 0 mg, carbohydrates 25 g, fiber 6 g, protein 8 g

# CHUCK'S HUMMUS

4 CUPS, 8 SERVINGS

This slightly less traditional hummus recipe was created by my husband, Chuck, who was feeling particularly creative one afternoon and came up with this sweet yet spicy dip.

2 15-ounce cans garbanzo beans, drained and rinsed

½ cup raisins

2 teaspoons crushed red pepper

1 teaspoon chopped garlic

3 teaspoons canola oil

2 teaspoons water

2 teaspoons soy sauce

juice of ½ lemon

Purée garbanzo beans, raisins, pepper, and garlic in a food processor, adding oil, water, soy sauce, and lemon juice as it processes. Purée until the mixture is light and fluffy.

Serve with pita bread cut into triangles, pita chips, or raw vegetables.

*Per serving:* calories 188, calories from fat 22, total fat 2 g, cholesterol 0 mg, carbohydrates 38 g, fiber 5 g, protein 5 g

# GARBANZO RAITA

3 CUPS, 10 SERVINGS

This fresh and light dipping sauce has lots of uses: Try it as a side for a spicy Middle Eastern dinner, as a dip with pita bread triangles, or as a cool refreshing dip with crudités.

---

2 cups cooked garbanzos, drained and rinsed

1 cup plain yogurt

1 small cucumber, peeled and sliced

2 tablespoons fresh lemon juice

2 tablespoons fresh chopped mint leaves (or 1 tablespoon dried)

2 cloves garlic, minced

pinch of sugar

salt and black pepper to taste

---

Place the garbanzos in a food processor and purée until smooth. Add yogurt and purée again. Add the cucumber and process again until the cucumber is finely chopped.

Place the bean mixture in a medium bowl and stir in the lemon juice, mint, garlic, and sugar.

Add salt and pepper to taste.

Refrigerate for at least 1 hour to allow flavors to blend.

*Per serving:* calories 79, calories from fat 9, total fat 1 g, cholesterol 1 mg, carbohydrates 14 g, fiber 2 g, protein 4 g

# CHICKPEA FALAFEL WITH ZESTY SAUCE

8 SERVINGS

These crispy balls of fried chickpea purée provide a great starter for any type of meal or an appetizer for a cocktail party. The dipping sauce provides just the right amount of spicy flavor.

---

2 14-ounce cans chickpeas, drained and rinsed

12 scallions, finely chopped

2 eggs

2 teaspoons ground turmeric

¼–½ teaspoon cayenne pepper

2 tablespoons soy sauce

1 tablespoon finely minced garlic

2 teaspoons ground cumin

2 tablespoons chopped fresh cilantro

oil for deep frying

---

Place the chickpeas and scallions in a food processor or blender and process until smooth. Add the eggs, turmeric, cayenne, soy sauce, garlic, cumin, and chopped cilantro. Process to mix.

Shape the chickpea mixture into 32 small balls.

Heat the oil for deep frying to 350° F. Deep fry the falafel in batches for 3 to 4 minutes or until golden brown.

Drain on paper towels. Place in a serving bowl and keep warm in a low oven.

Serve with dipping sauce

## Dipping Sauce

---

3 tablespoons mayonnaise

3 tablespoons sour cream

1 teaspoon Asian chili garlic sauce

3 tablespoons chopped fresh cilantro

---

Mix all of the above well. Garnish with a sprig of cilantro.

*Per serving:* calories 159, calories from fat 24, total fat 3 g, cholesterol 63 mg, carbohydrates 27 g, fiber 5 g, protein 8 g

# JENNIFER'S BEAN TOASTS

ABOUT 48 TOASTS

Jennifer—

I found this recipe stuck on your refrigerator. Thank you! As usual, everything that emerged from your kitchen was great (and garlicky).

—S.

2 15.5-ounce cans garbanzo beans, drained and rinsed

8 cloves garlic minced

1 tablespoon dried basil

1 tablespoon oregano

2 tablespoons extra virgin olive oil

1 tablespoon balsamic vinegar

black pepper to taste

¼ teaspoon crushed red pepper

1–1½ large French baguettes

extra olive oil for drizzling

Parmesan cheese

chopped fresh parsley for garnish

Preheat oven to 400° F.

Place beans, garlic, basil, oregano, olive oil, vinegar, black pepper, and crushed red pepper in a food processor and process until smooth or mash until well blended.

Slice French bread into slices ½-inch thick. Drizzle with olive oil and put a generous amount of bean mixture on top of each slice. Sprinkle each with Parmesan cheese. Bake in a preheated oven for 4 to 7 minutes or until cheese is melted and bean mixture starts to bubble.

Serve immediately on a warm platter and sprinkle the chopped parsley over all.

*Per serving:* calories 425, calories from fat 44, total fat 5 g, cholesterol 0 mg, carbohydrates 79 g, fiber 14 g, protein 17 g

# CHICKPEA POT STICKERS

32 POT STICKERS

If you are afraid of making little pastry-like appetizers because of the rolling procedures and time issues, you've got nothing to fear from these little morsels. The egg-roll wrappers used here make the pastry issue a breeze, and these can be done on a day when you have some free time and frozen to deep fry on the day you need them.

---

1 15.5-ounce can chickpeas, drained and rinsed

3 tablespoons olive oil

1 tablespoon sesame oil

2 teaspoons minced garlic

2 tablespoons soy sauce

1 tablespoon Asian chili garlic sauce (or less if you prefer less spice)

6 scallions, chopped (both white and green parts)

3 carrots, finely chopped in a food processor or blender

½ cup thinly sliced celery

8 egg-roll wrappers, cut into quarters

oil for deep frying

---

Place the chickpeas into a food processor or blender and process until finely chopped but with texture, not smooth.

In a large skillet, heat the olive and sesame oil. Add the garlic, soy sauce, and Asian chili garlic sauce.

Stir to heat and add the processed chickpeas. Stir in the scallions, chopped carrots, and celery. Stir until the mixture is heated through.

Place a generous teaspoon of the chickpea filling on each quarter of the egg-roll wrappers. Fold over into a triangle shape and use the tines of a fork dipped in water to press the edges together.

Heat oil for deep frying to 350° F. Fry small batches of the pot stickers at a time until golden brown. Remove from oil and place on a platter with paper towels to drain excess oil.

Serve hot with dipping sauce.

## Dipping Sauce

---

1 cup orange marmalade

3 tablespoons soy sauce

---

Mix together to create a simple yet perfect taste to complement these pot stickers.

*Per pot sticker:* calories 61, calories from fat 18, total fat 2 g, cholesterol 1 mg, carbohydrates 9 g, fiber 1 g, protein 2 g

# CRUNCHY ROASTED CECI NUTS

2 TO 6 SERVINGS (DEPENDING ON THE SIZE OF THE HANDFUL)

Bowls of these crunchy, tasty, and nutritious snacks will need to be replenished regularly—they'll disappear like popcorn.

---

2 cups cooked chickpeas, drained and rinsed

¼ cup extra virgin olive oil

¼ cup butter

3 teaspoons minced garlic

¼ teaspoon cayenne pepper

1 teaspoon onion salt

---

Preheat oven to 350° F.

Place the chickpeas in a mixing bowl.

In a small saucepan, melt the butter with the olive oil. Add the garlic, cayenne pepper, and onion salt. Stir to blend.

Pour butter mixture over the chickpeas and toss to completely coat. Spread the chickpeas out on a baking pan, just one layer deep.

Bake for 30 to 45 minutes, stirring often, until the chickpeas are golden and crunchy.

These can be served warm or at room temperature

*Per serving:* calories 239, calories from fat 154, total fat 18 g, cholesterol 21 mg, carbohydrates 18 g, fiber 3 g, protein 4 g

# Salads, Soups & Sides

## CHICKPEA AND COUSCOUS SALAD

6 SERVINGS

This light and lemony salad makes a great summertime lunch.

3 tablespoons canola oil

6 scallions, chopped (both white and green parts)

1 teaspoon minced garlic

1 teaspoon ground cumin

½ teaspoon coriander

1½ cups chicken broth (or vegetable broth)

1 cup couscous

1 15.5-ounce can chickpeas, drained and rinsed

2 tomatoes, finely chopped

1 cucumber, peeled and diced

¼ cup chopped fresh parsley

¼ cup chopped fresh mint

3 tablespoons fresh lemon juice

salt and freshly ground black pepper to taste

romaine lettuce

zest of 1 lemon, zested into long delicate shreds

toasted pine nuts

In a medium saucepan, heat the oil. Add the scallions and garlic. Stir in the cumin and coriander. Cook for 1 minute. Add the broth and bring to a boil.

Remove the pan from the heat and stir in the couscous. Cover and let stand for 10 minutes or until the liquid has been absorbed and couscous has swelled.

Transfer couscous to a large bowl. Stir in chickpeas, tomatoes, cucumber, parsley, mint, and lemon juice. Add salt and pepper to taste. Set aside for up to 1 hour to allow flavors to develop.

Line a large shallow salad bowl with the romaine leaves and spoon the couscous mixture over the top. Sprinkle with the toasted pine nuts and zest of lemon over the top.

*Per serving:* calories 311, calories from fat 78, total fat 9 g, cholesterol 0 mg, carbohydrates 48 g, fiber 9 g, protein 12 g

# CHICKPEA AND SPRING VEGETABLE SALAD

6 SERVINGS

This very solid salad could easily fill in as a main course. Springtime is perfect for improvisation, so feel free to fill in with whatever fresh and wonderful veggies you like.

---

1½ pounds baby red potatoes, halved

2 cups cooked chickpeas, drained and rinsed

1 cup grape tomatoes, halved

¾ cup walnut halves

2 tablespoons rice wine vinegar

1 tablespoon Dijon mustard

¼ cup olive oil

pinch of sugar or sweetener

8 ounces fresh young asparagus spears, trimmed

6 large scallions, trimmed to just above the white part (discard green part)

sea salt and fresh ground black pepper to taste

1 10-ounce bag baby spinach leaves

---

Place the potatoes in a saucepan. Cover with cold water and bring to a boil. Cook for 10 to 12 minutes or until tender. In a large bowl, combine chickpeas, tomatoes, and walnuts.

Combine the rice vinegar, mustard, olive oil, and sugar in a small bowl and whisk well.

Add the asparagus to the potatoes and cook for 3 minutes more. Drain the potatoes and asparagus well, rinse under cold running water, and drain again.

Depending on the size of the potatoes, you might want to quarter the halves.

Slice the scallions lengthwise in half to make long, delicate sections.

Add the asparagus, potatoes, and scallions to the bowl with the chickpea mixture. Pour the dressing over the salad and toss well. Add salt and pepper to taste.

Place the baby spinach in a large, flat salad bowl and top with the vegetable mixture.

*Per serving:* calories 391, calories from fat 173, total fat 20 g, cholesterol 0 mg, carbohydrates 46 g, fiber 9 g, protein 11 g

## CECI SALAD

4 SERVINGS

Serve this easy and tasty salad on its own or as a different addition to an antipasto tray. This was almost always seen at our family's expansive Christmas Eve buffets, surrounded by greens and roasted peppers along with the rest of the Italian world of wonderful Christmas foods.

1 19-ounce can garbanzos, drained and rinsed

1 large red onion, chopped

1 teaspoon minced garlic

1 teaspoon oregano

salt to taste

3 tablespoons chopped fresh parsley

2 tablespoons extra virgin olive oil

Combine all the ingredients in a large bowl and toss gently to mix. Chill for at least 1 hour to allow the flavors to blend.

*Per serving:* calories 236, calories from fat 74, total fat 8 g, cholesterol 0 mg, fiber 7 g, protein 7 g

# CECI BEAN SOUP

8 SERVINGS

Simple to make; delicious and nutritious to eat.

6 10-ounce cans ceci beans, drained and rinsed

2 tablespoons olive oil

1 cup chopped carrots

1 cup chopped celery

1 cup chopped onion

6 cups chicken broth (or vegetable broth)

2 cloves garlic, crushed

2 tablespoons chopped fresh parsley

½ head escarole, washed well and ripped

salt and pepper to taste

Mash or purée 3 cans of ceci beans, leaving the other 3 cans whole. Heat oil in a skillet and sauté the celery, onions, and carrots until just beginning to soften.

Heat the broth in a large soup pot and add the sautéed vegetables. Add both mashed and whole ceci beans, garlic, escarole, parsley, salt, and pepper.

Bring to a boil, reduce heat and simmer until escarole is cooked and the other vegetables are soft.

Perfect for a winter afternoon, when warmth and comfort are all that matters.

*Per serving:* calories 338, calories from fat 61, total fat 7 g, cholesterol 0 mg, carbohydrates 54 g, fiber 11 g, protein 16 g

# PASTA AND CHICKPEA SOUP

6 SERVINGS

Here is a soup that is easy, nutritious, Italian, and can be made on a moment's notice. And what a wonderful type of soup that is!

½ cup olive oil

6 cloves garlic, smashed

1 19-ounce can chickpeas, drained and rinsed

sea salt and freshly ground pepper to taste

4 cups chicken broth (or vegetable broth)

½ pound small pasta shells

¾ cup fresh grated Parmesan cheese

In a saucepan, heat oil over moderate heat. Add the garlic cloves and sauté, stirring until they are golden brown on all sides, about 2 minutes. Add the chickpeas, salt and pepper to taste, and cook, stirring, for 3 more minutes. Add the broth and bring to a boil. Reduce the heat and simmer, covered, for 20 minutes.

With a slotted spoon, remove about a quarter of the chickpeas and mash or purée with a fork or food processor. Return the puréed chickpeas to the soup and bring to a boil again, over moderate heat, stirring occasionally. Add the pasta and simmer, covered, until the pasta is *al dente*. Remove from heat and stir in the Parmesan cheese. Let stand for 2 to 3 minutes.

Serve with additional Parmesan cheese available for individual servings.

*Per serving:* calories 425, calories from fat 212, total fat 24 g, cholesterol 10 mg, carbohydrates 37 g, fiber 5 g, protein 16 g

# CREAMY SESAME GARBANZO AND SPINACH SOUP

4 SERVINGS

This is a deliciously thick, rich soup with a combination of spices that sets it apart from other cream soups. Add a baguette and salad, and you've got a complete meal.

3 tablespoons olive oil

2 tablespoons minced garlic

1 large onion, chopped

1 teaspoon ginger

2 teaspoons ground cumin

2 teaspoons coriander

6 cups chicken broth (or vegetable broth)

3 small (or 2 large) potatoes, peeled and diced

1 15.5-ounce can garbanzos, drained and rinsed

2 tablespoons cornstarch

1 cup heavy cream

3 tablespoons tahini (sesame paste)

8 ounces fresh spinach, ripped into small pieces

cayenne pepper to taste

salt and black pepper to taste

Heat the oil in a large soup pot and cook the garlic and onion until the onion starts to turn golden, about 5 minutes.

Stir in the ginger, cumin, and coriander.

Pour in the broth and add the diced potatoes to the soup pot. Bring to a boil and simmer for 10 minutes. Add the garbanzos and cook for another 8 to 10 minutes.

In a small bowl, combine the cornstarch, heavy cream, and tahini. Stir into the soup pot and add the spinach.

Bring to a boil once more, stirring constantly; reduce heat and simmer another 3 minutes. Add the cayenne pepper, salt, and black pepper to taste.

Serve at once, providing the cayenne pepper for individual additions.

*Per serving:* calories 535, calories from fat 268, total fat 31 g, cholesterol 41 mg, carbohydrates 49 g, fiber 9 g, protein 19 g

# ZUPPA DI ROMANA

4 SERVINGS

My father's family comes from a little town north of Rome, Italy. His claims that this soup was his family's version of a local classic might mean it was his version of the minute, as it was never quite the same way twice. It didn't matter, though, so this is just one delicious rendition.

---

½ cup extra virgin olive oil

1 teaspoon fresh rosemary

1 tablespoon minced garlic

2 tablespoons anchovy paste (or 3 anchovy filets, finely chopped)

1 tablespoon tomato paste diluted in ¼ cup water

3 cups cooked garbanzo beans, drained and rinsed

4 cups water

1 cup tubettini pasta

salt and pepper to taste

Parmesan cheese

4 sprigs fresh rosemary for garnish

---

Heat olive oil in a large soup pan and add rosemary, garlic, and anchovies. Brown well.

Add the diluted tomato paste and cook over low heat for 15 minutes.

Add the garbanzo beans and 4 cups of water. Bring to a boil and add tubettini pasta. Reduce heat and cook for 8 minutes or until pasta is tender.

Season with salt and pepper.

Have the Parmesan cheese available for individual additions to the soup, and garnish each serving with a sprig of fresh rosemary.

Italian bread should actually be listed as an ingredient, since it is essential to this soup for dipping.

*Per serving:* calories 602, calories from fat 278, total fat 32 g, cholesterol 18 mg, carbohydrates 62 g, fiber 9 g, protein 19 g

# SPICY GARBANZOS AND WALNUTS

4 SERVINGS

This preparation can be used as a side dish with a multitude of cuisine types and dishes. The heat depends on how heavy-handed you want to be with the crushed red pepper flakes...

3 teaspoons extra virgin olive oil

1 clove of garlic, minced

crushed red pepper to taste

¼ cup finely chopped walnuts

2 cups cooked garbanzo beans, drained and rinsed

2 tablespoons soy sauce

2 teaspoons water

¼ cup finely chopped fresh parsley

Heat the olive oil in a large skillet or wok. Add the garlic and red pepper flakes and sauté for 2 minutes. Add the chopped walnuts and garbanzo beans and toss to coat. Add the soy sauce along with the water and cover and cook for 5 minutes. Stir in the parsley.

Be careful with the red pepper flakes. A little provides a lot of heat. I suggest a light sprinkle for the more delicate palate and up to 1 teaspoon for a heartier mouth.

*Per serving:* calories 221, calories from fat 82, total fat 10 g, cholesterol 0 mg, carbohydrates 28 g, fiber 6 g, protein 7 g

# HOT AND SPICY GARBANZOS AND CAULIFLOWER

4 SERVINGS

This beautifully colored side dish could also serve two as a main course. An Indian flatbread or basmati rice would fill it in nicely, along with a cucumber and yogurt raita.

6 tablespoons peanut oil

2 teaspoons ground cumin

1 teaspoon coriander

1 teaspoon ground turmeric

¼ teaspoon cayenne pepper

2 fresh green chilies, seeded and finely chopped

1 large cauliflower, cut into small florets

¼ cup water

2 cups cooked garbanzos

2 teaspoons cumin seeds

3 garlic cloves, cut into thin shreds

2 tablespoons finely chopped fresh cilantro

sea salt to taste

Heat 3 tablespoons of the peanut oil in a large skillet. Add the cumin, coriander, turmeric, cayenne, and chopped chilies. Let the spices sizzle for 3 to 5 seconds. Add the cauliflower and ¼ cup of water. Cook over medium heat, stirring constantly, about 6 minutes or until cauliflower is softened. Add the garbanzos and cook for another 2 to 3 minutes, stirring constantly. Season with salt and remove from heat.

Heat the remaining 3 tablespoons of peanut oil in a small skillet. Add the cumin seeds and garlic shreds and cook until lightly browned. Pour over the cauliflower mixture. Top with the chopped cilantro.

Serve immediately.

*Per serving:* calories 443, calories from fat 198, total fat 23 g, cholesterol 0 mg, carbohydrates 53 g, fiber 15 g, protein 15 g

# CHICKPEA GRAVY

6 SERVINGS

This is a very healthy and unique topping for those of you who like a nice gravy over potatoes or rice, or with biscuits for a Southern-style breakfast.

1 15.5-ounce can chickpeas, drained and rinsed

1 cup chicken broth (or vegetable broth)

1 tablespoon tamari sauce

1 teaspoon minced garlic

½ small onion, finely minced

black pepper, to taste

Place all ingredients in a food processor or blender and process until smooth and creamy. Transfer to a saucepan and bring to a simmer over medium heat. Cook for 8 to 10 minutes.

*Per serving:* calories 96, calories from fat 9, total fat 1 g, cholesterol 0 mg, carbohydrates 17 g, fiber 3 g, protein 5 g

# Main Dishes

. . . . . . . . . . . . . . . . . . . . . . . . . . . .

## LINGUINI WITH CHICKPEAS AND ANCHOVIES

8 SERVINGS

In our earlier sailing days, my friend Pete Rinaldi and I had silent (and some not so silent) contests over who could feed the most people the best-tasting meal, cooking in the smallest pot in the least amount of time, with the limited ingredients one could find in the smallest of kitchens—the galley of a boat. This recipe would be it. ("Hey, Pete: I win!")

2 tablespoons extra virgin olive oil

3 cloves garlic

1 small tin anchovies

1 quart tomato sauce, prepared or homemade

1 15.5-ounce can chickpeas, drained and rinsed

¼ cup chopped fresh parsley

1 pound fettuccini pasta

Parmesan cheese

Heat the olive oil in a 2-quart saucepan and brown the garlic cloves. Discard the garlic (sad but true). Add the anchovies to the hot oil and mash with a fork. Pour the tomato sauce over the anchovies and stir to blend well. Add the chickpeas and bring sauce to a boil. Reduce heat and simmer for 45 minutes. Stir in parsley and cook for 10 more minutes.

Cook the fettuccini according to package directions. Drain well.

Place the fettuccini on a large platter and top with the sauce mixture.

Have Parmesan cheese available for topping individual servings along with some extra chopped parsley.

Italian bread and a crisp green salad make for a very happy crew.

*Per serving:* calories 339, calories from fat 53, total fat 6 g, cholesterol 9 mg, carbohydrates 58 g, fiber 6 g, protein 14 g

# MOUSSAKA

4 TO 6 SERVINGS

Garbanzo beans substitute for the ground lamb in this Greek dish. But purists, take heart: The garbanzos are a delicious and low-fat replacement. The dish loses nothing in flavor but gains points for the health-conscious eater.

---

1 large eggplant, thinly sliced

salt to taste

2 tablespoons olive oil

1 large onion, sliced

3 cloves garlic, minced

4 ripe tomatoes, chopped

4 tablespoons chopped fresh basil

2 teaspoons dried oregano

¼ cup dry white wine

3 eggs, lightly beaten

1 cup plain yogurt

1 cup cooked garbanzo beans, drained and rinsed

4 tablespoons freshly grated Parmesan cheese

---

Preheat oven to 300° F.

Place eggplant slices in a colander and sprinkle with salt. Place a plate to weigh them down and let sit for 30 minutes for excess water to drain.

Blot eggplant slices with paper towels and place on a baking sheet. Bake at 300° F until flesh can be pierced easily with a fork, about 15 minutes.

While eggplant bakes, warm olive oil in a skillet over medium heat. Add onion and sauté until soft, about 3 to 5 minutes. Add garlic, tomatoes, basil, oregano, and wine. Cook until tomatoes soften, about 10 minutes.

Place baked eggplant in a lightly greased 9 x 12-inch baking dish. Increase oven temp to 350° F.

Mix yogurt with the eggs.

Spread garbanzos over the eggplant. Top with the beaten egg and yogurt mixture. Spoon tomato mixture over the top. Sprinkle with the Parmesan cheese and bake for 45 minutes.

Serve hot.

A dry Greek wine, a salad with Greek black olives and feta cheese, a crusty roll, and the theme from *Zorba the Greek* makes for a wonderful dinner!

*Per serving:* calories 250, calories from fat 95, total fat 11 g, cholesterol 151 mg, carbohydrates 27 g, fiber 6 g, protein 11 g

# GARBANZOS, PASTA, SPINACH, AND CHEESE

6 SERVINGS

This is a meal. In terms of nutrition, it is complete and well balanced and takes no more than 20 minutes to prepare. Perfect for a weeknight or any meal when time is tight but nutrition still important (which should basically be always).

12 ounces rotini pasta

2 10-ounce bags fresh baby spinach leaves

2 tablespoons extra virgin olive oil

3 cloves garlic, finely minced

1 19-ounce can of garbanzos, drained and rinsed

red pepper flakes to taste

1 cup shredded fontina cheese

Bring a large pot of lightly salted water to a boil. Add the pasta and cook according to package directions for *al dente*. Add the spinach to the pasta water. Scoop out and reserve ½ cup of the cooking water. Immediately drain the pasta and spinach in a colander.

Heat the olive oil in a large skillet over medium-high heat. Add the garlic and sauté for about 2 minutes. Add the garbanzos and red pepper flakes and cook for 1 more minute and remove from heat.

Combine pasta mixture, garbanzo beans, and cheese in a large bowl. Stir in the reserved pasta cooking water and serve immediately. Have the red pepper flakes on hand for those who like it extra hot.

If you like, you can round this out with an arugula salad.

*Per serving:* calories 472, calories from fat 120, total fat 14 g, cholesterol 26 mg, carbohydrates 68 g, fiber 8 g, protein 20 g

# PASTA AGLIO, OLIO (Pasta with Garlic and Olive Oil)

8 SERVINGS

This is a variation on a classic Italian pasta dish. The sauce has an intense garlic flavor and the chickpeas provide the once-missing protein and fiber.

---

½ cup olive oil

4–5 large garlic cloves

½ stick butter

1 cup cooked chickpeas, drained and rinsed

¼ cup fresh parsley, finely chopped

hot pepper flakes to taste

1 pound long pasta (thin spaghetti, capellini, or vermicelli)

½ cup freshly grated Parmesan cheese

---

Heat olive oil and garlic in a medium sized skillet. As the cloves start to brown, pierce them with a fork and mash slightly to release the full flavor. Reduce heat. Add the butter and melt. Add the chickpeas, parsley, and hot pepper flakes. Stir to mix and cook until chickpeas are warmed through. Remove from heat.

Cook the pasta according to package directions. Drain and top with the oil and butter sauce. Add the Parmesan cheese and toss to coat.

Have extra Parmesan and hot pepper flakes available for individual tastes.

*Per serving:* calories 948, calories form fat 197, total fat 22 g, cholesterol 20 mg, carbohydrates 164 g, fiber 1 g, protein 22 g

# GARBANZOS FRITOS (Fried Garbanzos)

4 SERVINGS

This is a Puerto Rican protein-packed breakfast that Ada Rodriguez nourishes her family with on weekends. The original recipe calls for bacon, but I have found that the soy bacon product is quite acceptable in replacing the taste and texture that real bacon provided.

12 ounces soy bacon product (e.g., "Fakin' Bacon")

1 tablespoon olive oil

1 onion, cut into small pieces

1 green pepper, diced

1 15.5-ounce can garbanzo beans, drained and rinsed

1 envelope Sazón con color (anato)

4 eggs

Cut the bacon into square pieces and sauté in a large skillet until almost golden. Remove the bacon from the pan.

Add 1 tablespoon of olive oil and heat. Add and stir-fry the onions and green pepper over medium heat until soft, about 2 to 3 minutes. Add the garbanzo beans, Sazón, and bacon pieces. Continue to sauté for another 3 to 5 minutes, stirring occasionally.

Break the 4 eggs over the bean mixture, keeping them separate in four corners. Cover and cook until eggs are set.

Serve immediately with a tostada (toast) made from the fresh water bread similar to that which the Puerto Ricans make best. You can find these wonderful loaves in any grocery store bakery; just slice thickly, toast, and enjoy.

*Per serving:* calories 270, calories from fat 94, total fat 11 g, cholesterol 247 mg, carbohydrates 31 g, fiber 6 g, protein 13 g

# FARFALLE WITH CHICKPEAS, ZUCCHINI, AND TOMATOES  8 SERVINGS

Farfalle is the bow-tie pasta found in the pasta section of any grocery store. Their shape lends to the visual appeal of this colorful, flavorful, and nutritious main course.

12 ounces farfalle

2 tablespoons extra virgin olive oil

2 cups chopped red onion

4 cloves garlic, minced

3 cups of grape or cherry tomatoes, halved

1 medium zucchini, cut into 1-inch pieces

1 19-ounce can chickpeas, drained and rinsed

½ cup chopped parsley

½ cup grated Parmesan cheese

Cook pasta in lightly salted boiling water. Reserve ¼ cup of the cooking liquid, then drain the pasta well.

Heat oil in a large skillet over medium-high heat. Add onions and garlic and cook until soft, for about 5 minutes.

Add tomatoes, zucchini, and chickpeas. Cook about 6 minutes or until vegetables are cooked through.

Add the reserved cooling liquid to the skillet; stir and toss with the pasta. Stir in the parsley and Parmesan cheese.

Try this with a hearty loaf of bread and a dip of olive oil and red pepper flakes. Conveniently, either red or white wine will go well with this.

*Per serving:* calories 781, calories from fat 509, total fat 58 g, cholesterol 5 mg, carbohydrates 55 g, fiber 6 g, protein 13 g

# CUCCIA (Chickpeas and Wheat Kernels)

6 TO 8 SERVINGS

Again, the wonder combination of beans and grain, creating the perfect protein, comes into play in this dish that could serve as breakfast, lunch, or dessert.

½ pound dried chickpeas

1 pound wheat kernels

2½–3 quarts warm water

1 tablespoon salt

Wash the chickpeas and wheat kernels with cold water and drain; cover with cold water and soak 4 hours or overnight. Drain and rinse. Place in a large kettle and stir in the warm water and salt. Bring to a boil, lower heat, cover, and simmer slowly for 1 to 1½ hours, or until chickpeas and kernels are tender but firm.

Here's where you can get creative. This can be served hot, at room temperature, or cold.

For breakfast, heat the cuccia and add butter, milk, and brown sugar. Stir in whatever fruit appeals to you.

For a hearty soup, heat the cuccia and add ¼ cup olive oil, ½ cup chopped parsley, fresh ground black pepper to taste, and maybe a squeeze of lemon.

For dessert, serve this cold with whipped cream, sugar, and cinnamon. Top with strawberries, raspberries, bananas, or whatever is seasonal and appeals to you.

*Per serving:* calories 192, calories from fat 10, total fat 1 g, cholesterol 0 mg, carbohydrates 39 g, fiber 7 g, protein 9 g

# CHANA MASALA (Braised Garbanzos with Spicy Sauce)

4 SERVINGS

The garbanzo returns to its original forum of Middle Eastern cuisine. An exotic combination of spices and flavors give you a glimpse into the world of Arabian night dinners.

6 tablespoons light olive oil

2 tablespoons cumin seeds

½ teaspoon dried thyme

2 teaspoons ground coriander

½ teaspoon ground turmeric

1 fresh green chili, finely chopped

2 cups finely chopped onion

4 tablespoons grated fresh ginger

2 large tomatoes, peeled, seeded, and chopped

4 tablespoons tomato paste

4 cups cooked garbanzos, drained and rinsed

fresh ground black pepper and coarse sea salt

## Garnish

½ cup chopped cilantro leaves

½ cup finely chopped onion

¼ cup chopped green chilies

In a large pan, over medium heat, heat the olive oil. Add the cumin seeds and sauté for 2 minutes.

Add thyme, coriander, turmeric, chili, onion, and ginger.

Cook, stirring often, until the onion turns light brown, about 8 minutes. Add the tomatoes, tomato paste, and garbanzos. Lower heat and cover. Simmer for about 15 minutes until the sauce is very thick. Season with the black pepper and sea salt.

Transfer to a large, warmed platter and top with cilantro and chopped onion.

Pass the chilies separately for individual toppings.

*Per serving:* calories 553, calories from fat 212, total fat 24 g, cholesterol 0 mg, carbohydrates 71 g, fiber 14 g, protein 15 g

# GARBANZOS ALLA JARDINERA

4 TO 6 SERVINGS

This is one of Julio Perez's milder creations. Julio lives in Boqueron, Puerto Rico, and has as much fun with food as he does with people. He creates dishes like an impressionist might paint—with wild fervor. His experimentations produce some of the most unlikely combinations of flavors that, oddly enough, always taste wonderful.

---

½ stick salted butter

4 tablespoons extra virgin olive oil

1 medium onion, chopped

4 cloves garlic, minced

1 medium red pepper, chopped

1 medium green bell pepper, chopped

1 large tomato, diced

1 15.5-ounce can garbanzo beans

1 small jar roasted red peppers, chopped

½ cup chopped pitted black olives

2 envelopes Sazón con achote y cilantro

3–4 slices Swiss cheese

¾ cup grated Parmesan cheese

---

Preheat oven to 450° F.

Melt the butter in a large skillet. Add the olive oil and heat. Stir in the onion, garlic, red and green pepper, and tomato. Stir-fry until the vegetables are tender. Add the garbanzos, roasted red peppers, olives, and Sazón Criollo seasoning. Stir and cook 1 to 2 more minutes.

Pour the mixture into a 9-inch pie dish. Layer the Swiss cheese, so it completely covers the top. Top with the Parmesan cheese.

Bake until the cheese is melted and bubbly.

Serve this with a crisp, cold green salad and a crisp, cold, dry white wine.

*Per serving:* calories 401, calories from fat 244, total fat 28 g, cholesterol 48 mg, carbohydrates 24 g, fiber 5 g, protein 15 g

# GREEN GARBANZO GUMBO

10 TO 12 SERVINGS

The garbanzo does New Orleans in this rich and delicious version of a Creole classic. Even minus the ham hocks usually used for seasoning, this version maintains a gutsy down-South flavor.

---

1 bunch spinach

1 bunch arugula

1 bunch escarole

1 medium-size green cabbage

8 cups water

8 cups chicken broth (or vegetable broth)

3 tablespoons butter or shortening

1 tablespoon olive oil

6 tablespoons flour

½ bunch scallions, chopped (both white and green parts)

1 green bell pepper, chopped

3 stalks celery, thickly chopped

1 large white or yellow onion, chopped

1 tablespoon minced garlic

1 bunch flat leaf parsley, chopped

1 15-ounce can stewed tomatoes

2 15.5-ounce cans garbanzo beans, drained and rinsed

1½ cups okra slices (frozen can be used)

1 cup fresh or frozen corn kernels

2 teaspoons paprika

2 bay leaves

4 sprigs fresh thyme

2 whole cloves

sea salt and fresh ground black pepper, to taste

cayenne pepper to taste

4–5 dashes Tabasco sauce (Really—use Tabasco sauce, not just any hot sauce. Tabasco adds to the authentic Louisiana flavor.)

5–6 cups cooked white rice

---

Wash the spinach, arugula, and escarole well and remove stems and hard centers. Chop them all finely. Chop the green cabbage, discarding the core.

Combine the water and broth in a large soup pot and boil the spinach, arugula, escarole, and green cabbage for about 1 hour. Set aside.

In a large stock pot, melt the butter and olive oil. Add flour and stir until mixture starts to thicken. Add the scallions, green pepper, celery, onion, and garlic. Sauté over medium heat for 8 to 10 minutes. Stir in the chopped parsley.

Pour in the greens and broth mixture, stewed tomatoes, and garbanzo beans. Add the remaining ingredients and simmer on low heat for 1 to 1½ hours more. Add more water if it looks like it is thickening too much.

On the last simmer hour, play with the spices. Add more of whatever your palate tells you to.

Place the cooked rice in the bottom of each individual serving bowl. Ladle the gumbo over the rice and serve up the best of the South to your deserving guests.

I do believe ice-cold beer goes very nicely with a spicy gumbo.

*Per serving:* calories 330, calories from fat 59, total fat 7 g, cholesterol 8 mg, carbohydrates 56 g, fiber 8 g, protein 14 g

# CHICKPEA AND EGGPLANT STEW

6 SERVINGS

As you've probably noticed, different beans seem more at home in certain cuisines than others. The chickpea is most comfortable in Middle Eastern cooking, and this recipe is a fine example.

3 large eggplants, cubed

1 cup chickpeas, soaked overnight

¼ cup extra virgin olive oil

2 tablespoons minced garlic

2 large onions, chopped

½ teaspoon ground cumin

½ teaspoon cinnamon

½ teaspoon ground coriander

½ teaspoon ground turmeric

2 large zucchinis, cubed

3 14-ounce cans chopped tomatoes

kosher salt and black pepper to taste

fresh cilantro or fresh parsley sprigs for garnish

Place the eggplant in a colander and sprinkle with salt. Set in a sink with a plate over the eggplant for weight and let sit for 30 minutes for the excess liquid to drain. Rinse eggplant and pat dry with paper towels.

Drain and rinse the chickpeas. Place in a medium saucepan with enough water to cover. Bring to a boil and simmer for 90 minutes or until tender. Drain and rinse again.

Heat the olive oil in a saucepan. Add garlic and onion and cook until the onions are soft. Add the cumin, cinnamon, coriander, and turmeric and stir. Add the eggplant and zucchini, stirring again to coat. Cook for 5 minutes. Add the tomatoes and cooked chickpeas. Season with salt and pepper.

Cover and simmer for 25 minutes.

## Topping

3 tablespoons olive oil

2 large onions, sliced

2 garlic cloves, sliced

1 teaspoon sugar

Heat the olive oil and add onions, garlic, and sugar. Sauté until onions are golden and crisp.

Serve the stew over basmati rice; top with the crisp onions and garlic. Garnish the plates with either fresh cilantro or fresh parsley sprigs.

Use an Indian flatbread for scooping up this delicious dinner.

*Per serving:* calories 343, calories from fat 97, total fat 11 g, cholesterol 0 mg, carbohydrates 56 g, fiber 15 g, protein 12 g

# CHICKPEA AFRICAN STEW

6 SERVINGS

This recipe is a study in simplicity, yet exotic and delicious.

---

4 kohlrabis or parsnips, peeled and cut into chunks

½ cup uncooked couscous

1 onion, chopped

¼ cup raisins

2 sweet potatoes, peeled and cut into chunks

1 teaspoon ground coriander

1 teaspoon ground turmeric

3 small zucchini, sliced into ½-inch slices

½ teaspoon ground cinnamon

4 large tomatoes, chopped

½ teaspoon ground ginger

½ teaspoon ground cumin

2 cups cooked chickpeas, drained and rinsed

3 cups water

---

Combine all ingredients in a large saucepan. Bring to a boil and reduce the heat. Simmer until vegetables are tender, about 35 to 40 minutes.

*Per serving:* calories 294, calories from fat 15, total fat 2 g, cholesterol 0 mg, carbohydrates 64 g, fiber 11 g, protein 10 g

# NORTH AFRICAN GARBANZO AND FAVA BEAN STEW

8 SERVINGS

The ground cinnamon and coriander add a romantic flavor to this hearty two-bean dish.

½ pound fava beans, rinsed and sorted

½ pound garbanzo beans, rinsed and sorted

8 cups chicken broth (or vegetable broth)

10 cups water

4 tablespoons extra virgin olive oil

2 tablespoons butter

2 large onions, chopped

2 tablespoons minced garlic

1 tablespoon ground coriander

3 teaspoons ground cumin

2 teaspoons ground cinnamon

6 cups chopped tomatoes

½ cup chopped fresh parsley

Soak beans in water to cover for 24 hours, changing water twice. Drain and rinse beans and place in a large soup pot.

Add the broth and 8 cups of the water. Bring to a boil over high heat. Reduce heat and simmer for 1½ to 2 hours or until beans are tender. Add a little more water as needed during cooking time if all liquid is absorbed before they are done.

In a large skillet, heat olive oil and butter over high heat. Add onions, garlic, coriander, cumin, and cinnamon, stirring constantly for 5 minutes. Add the remaining 2 cups water.

Reduce heat and cook for 15 minutes over medium heat, stirring frequently. Add to the cooked beans in the soup pot along with the tomatoes. Bring to a boil over high heat, reduce heat to medium, and cook for 30 to 35 minutes, until mixture has thickened.

Serve immediately, garnishing each serving with chopped parsley.

Serve this stew in a shallow bowl with a warm Middle Eastern bread. It is also excellent over basmati rice. This is one of those dishes that improves with age, so feel free to make this a day or two ahead of a planned dinner. The extra time on the day you serve it is always a bonus.

*Per serving:* calories 325, calories from fat 118, total fat 13 g, cholesterol 8 mg, carbohydrates 37 g, fiber 11 g, protein 17 g

# CHICKPEA FRITTATA

4 SERVINGS

Frittatas are basically large and hearty omelets, filled with vegetables. The vegetables you use are as interchangeable as the season and your taste.

3 tablespoons canola oil

1 teaspoon sesame oil

1 red onion, chopped

½ red bell pepper, diced

½ green bell pepper, diced

1 celery stalk, diced

1 plum tomato, diced

1 14-ounce can chickpeas, drained and rinsed

8 eggs

sea salt and freshly ground black pepper to taste

2 tablespoons sesame seeds

Heat both oils together in a 12-inch flameproof omelet pan. Add red onion, red and green pepper, celery, and the plum tomato. Cook until the vegetables just begin to soften. Add the chickpeas and cook for 2 to 3 more minutes.

In a mixing bowl, whisk the eggs until foamy, add salt and pepper, then pour the mixture over the bean mixture in the omelet pan.

Gently stir to distribute the vegetables. Cover the pan and cook over low heat for 6 to 8 minutes.

Sprinkle the sesame seed over the frittata. Place under a broiler flame until the sesame seeds brown, about 2 to 3 minutes. The broiler heat also lifts the frittata.

Cut the frittata into 4 wedges and serve warm. For a simple dinner or lunch, add a fresh, crisp, green salad and a dry cold wine. For a hearty breakfast, serve with some cold grapes and fresh-squeezed orange juice.

*Per serving:* calories 450, calories from fat 238, total fat 27 g, cholesterol 493 mg, carbohydrates 32 g, fiber 7 g, protein 21 g

# Desserts

## COCONUT WALNUT CHICKPEA PIE

6 TO 8 SERVINGS

My friends were very relieved to taste this pie during the test-kitchen days of putting this book together. They were getting tired of being the bean guinea pigs and thought this one was not part of the project. It is rich and wonderful and very pecan pie-ish in texture. I couldn't bring myself to tell them otherwise. Sorry, guys.

---

2 cups cooked chickpeas, drained and rinsed

¼ cup margarine

4 eggs

2 cups dark brown sugar

1 cup coconut milk or cream

1 tablespoon vanilla

1½ cup coarsely chopped walnuts

¾ cup flaked coconut

1 9-inch deep-dish pie crust, uncooked

---

Preheat oven to 350° F.

Purée the chickpeas in a food processor. Add the margarine. Add the eggs one at a time, processing until the mixture is very smooth and creamy. Transfer the chickpea mixture into a mixing bowl. Add the brown sugar and coconut milk and beat until blended.

Stir in the walnuts and coconut.

Pour into the pie crust and bake in a preheated oven for 50 to 60 minutes or until a knife inserted in the center comes out clean.

Serve warm or at room temperature with a little whipped cream.

*Per serving:* calories 700, calories from fat 331, total fat 39 g, cholesterol 129 mg, carbohydrates 81 g, fiber 5 g, protein 12 g

# CIAMBALONI

6 TO 8 SERVINGS

Here's a denser, healthier version of an Italian classic dessert cake. There is no flour in this reproduction, and the result is a very moist, rich, flavorful cake that could just as easily be served for a holiday as a Monday night.

---

1 15.5-ounce can garbanzo beans, drained and rinsed

4 eggs

1 cup Splenda or sugar

1 teaspoon baking powder

½ teaspoon baking soda

pinch of salt

2 teaspoons anise flavoring

½ cup chopped cherries

¼ cup chocolate chips

1 teaspoon anise seeds

confectioners' sugar (optional)

---

Preheat oven to 350° F. Grease a 9 x 9-inch square pan.

Place the garbanzo beans in a food processor and purée until almost smooth. Add the eggs, one at a time, processing after each addition. Add the sugar and purée until creamy.

Add the baking powder, baking soda, salt, and anise flavor and process just to mix well.

Gently stir in the cherries, chocolate chips, and anise seeds.

Pour batter into the prepared pan and place on center rack of the oven for 30 minutes or until a knife inserted in the center comes out clean.

Allow cake to cool and, if desired, sprinkle with confectioners' sugar.

*Per serving:* calories 254, calories from fat 45, total fat 5 g, cholesterol 123 mg, carbohydrates 47 g, fiber 3 g, protein 7 g

# PUMPKIN PIE

6 TO 8 SERVINGS

Try this one out for your next Thanksgiving meal. No one will blink an eye. They might be too full to eat it, but they'll force themselves to anyway, because it is soooo good. And they'll never know it's sugar free, high fiber, high protein, and low fat.

---

1 cup cooked garbanzo beans, drained and rinsed

2 eggs

1 12-ounce can light evaporated milk

1 teaspoon cinnamon

½ teaspoon cloves

¼ teaspoon nutmeg

1 cup Splenda (or 1 cup sugar)

1 cup canned pumpkin

1 9-inch deep-dish pie crust, uncooked

---

Preheat oven to 425° F.

Place the garbanzo beans into a food processor or blender and purée. Add the eggs and process until smooth and creamy.

Transfer bean mixture to a large mixing bowl, add the evaporated milk, and beat to blend. Add cinnamon, cloves, nutmeg, and Splenda or sugar. Mix well. Add the pumpkin and stir to mix well again.

Pour into the pie crust and bake at 425° F for 15 minutes. Reduce oven heat to 350° F. Bake for 40 to 50 minutes more or until a knife inserted in the center comes out clean. Let cool on a wire rack for 2 hours.

The finishing touch? Whipped cream, of course.

*Per serving:* calories 186, calories from fat 64, total fat 7 g, cholesterol 63 mg, carbohydrates 23 g, fiber 2 g, protein 8 g

# CINNAMON GARBANZO BREAD

12 SLICES

This slightly sweet breakfast yeast bread borrows the nutlike flavor of the garbanzo bean and blends it with cinnamon to create a dense and delicious start to the day. It works very well in a bread machine, too.

---

1 cup warm milk (about 100–110° F)

1 package active dry yeast

3 tablespoons brown sugar (divided use)

1 cup cooked garbanzo beans, drained and rinsed

2 teaspoons canola oil

3 cups bread flour

¼ teaspoon salt

1 tablespoon vital wheat gluten

1 tablespoon cinnamon

---

Preheat oven to 350° F.

Place the garbanzo beans into a food processor or blender and process until finely chopped, not puréed.

Pour the warm milk in a small bowl and add the yeast and 1 tablespoon of the brown sugar. Stir and set aside for about 10 minutes until the top begins to foam.

In a large mixing bowl, combine the garbanzo beans, oil, flour, salt, wheat gluten, cinnamon, and remaining 2 tablespoons of brown sugar.

Pour in the yeast and milk mixture and stir well to blend into a soft dough.

Knead the dough until smooth and elastic.

Set in a greased bowl and let rise for 1 hour or until double in bulk.

Punch down and let rise again for 1 hour more.

Shape into a loaf and place on a greased cookie sheet; cover and let rise for 30 minutes.

Place in preheated oven and bake for 45 minutes or until golden brown and sounds hollow when you tap it.

Serve warm with butter, which is probably as close to heaven as you will get first thing in the morning. This also makes the best toast you've ever had, so either way, enjoy!

*Per slice:* calories 171, calories from fat 15, total fat 2 g, cholesterol 2 mg, carbohydrates 33 g, fiber 2 g, protein 5 g

# WALNUT CHOCOLATE CHIP GARBANZO CAKE

ABOUT 18 PIECES

Nothing about this cake even whispers beans. The nutty flavor of the garbanzo blends in with the walnuts, and the chocolate chips pull it all together.

---

1 15.5-ounce can garbanzo beans, drained and rinsed

3 tablespoons water

1 stick of butter

2 cups brown sugar

2 eggs

1 tablespoon vanilla

1 teaspoon baking soda

1 teaspoon baking powder

2 cups flour

¼ teaspoon salt

1 cup finely chopped walnuts

1 cup chocolate chips

---

Preheat oven to 350° F.

Place the garbanzo beans in a food processor with 3 tablespoons water and process until smooth.

With a mixer, blend the butter and brown sugar until fluffy. Add the eggs and beat again. Add vanilla, baking soda, baking powder, flour, and salt and beat to mix. Add the puréed garbanzo beans and beat again. Stir in the walnuts and chocolate chips.

Pour batter into a 9 x 13-inch cake pan. Bake for 30 to 35 minutes or until a knife inserted in the center of the cake comes out clean.

Dust with confectioners' sugar if you like.

This is a great anytime cake when you need to sneak a little extra nutrition into your life and not have it taste like you are.

*Per piece:* calories 319, calories from fat 113, total fat 13 g, cholesterol 41 mg, carbohydrates 47 g, fiber 3 g, protein 5 g

# Red Beans

# Red Beans

## Kidney · Pinto · Pink · Small Red · Adzuki

*B*lack *beans are black,* white beans are white, but red beans run the gamut from deep burgundy (the kidney bean), to red-and-white-speckled beans (the pinto bean), to pink (um, the pink bean). Members of the red bean family used in these next recipes include the kidney bean, its relative the pink bean, small red beans, pinto beans, and adzuki beans.

Kidney beans and small red beans are basically interchangeable in any recipe. The kidney bean, so named for its curved, kidney-like shape, is a glossy burgundy color. It's larger than most beans, and, along with the smaller, redder, not-so-kidney-shaped small red bean, is among the most popular beans in the United States. Both of these varieties pick up flavors well and are excellent for adding to stews and marinating in salads, one of these being the famous three-bean salad. But if you are cooking them with tomatoes or sauce, please remember to precook the beans, as the acids in the tomato will prevent the bean from fully softening. (See Beans Done Right on p. xii)

A Mexican relative of the kidney bean, the pinto bean is a medium-size hybrid whose name comes from the Spanish word for "painted." The pinto has a medium-brown shell with darker spotted markings. Pintos blend especially well with limes and jalapeños or chili flavors.

They have a very smooth texture, so they make an excellent purée for soup bases or refrying.

The adzuki bean is a favorite in both Japanese and Chinese cuisines. These are small beans of a deep ruby color and a seam of white on the edge. Although they belong to the red bean family, they are not commonly grown in the United States. These beans are very easy to digest and have a distinctive flavor quite unlike any of the other bean families. Smaller than most beans, they cook faster. Adzuki beans are higher in nutrients than most beans and are very popular in the macrobiotic diet.

## Nutritional values for 1 cup of cooked beans

### Kidney Beans

Calories 225   Protein 15.3 g   Carbohydrates 40.4 g   Total Fat 0.88 g   Fiber 11.3 g
Iron 5.2 mg   Magnesium 80 mg   Folate 229 mcg   Calcium 78 mg

### Small Red Beans

Calories 226   Protein 16 g   Carbohydrates 40 g   Fiber 8 g   Folate 230 mcg
Calcium 50 mg   Iron 6 mg   Total fat 0.10 g

### Pinto Beans

Calories 234   Protein 14.0 g   Carbohydrates 43.8 g   Total Fat 0.89 g   Fiber 14.7 g
Iron 4.5 mg   Potassium 800 mg   Selenium 12 mcg   Folate 294 mcg   Calcium 82 mg

### Adzuki Beans

Calories 294   Protein 17.3 g   Carbohydrates 57 g   Total Fat 0.23 g   Fiber 16.8 g
Iron 4.6 mg   Magnesium 120 mg   Potassium 1,223 mg   Zinc 4.0 mg   Folate 278 mcg
Calcium 86 mg

## APPETIZERS

*Stuffed Mushrooms*

*Curried Citrus Dip*

*Dean's Beans*

*Red Bean Pâté*

*Stuffed Celery*

## SALADS, SOUPS & SIDES

*Bulgur and Red Bean Salad*

*Red and Green Bean Salad*

*Red Bean and Pickle Salad*

*Kidney Bean Salad, a.k.a. Three-Bean Salad*

*Southwest Three-Bean Salad*

*Red Potato Salad*

*White Tuna and Kidney Beans*

*Confetti Salad*

*Beet and Bean Borscht*

*Adzuki Soup*

*Red Bean Soup*

*Three Chili and Bean Soup*

*Barbeque Calico Beans*

## MAIN DISHES

*Chuck's Resurrected Red Beans*

*Ratatouille*

*Frijoles con Chiles y Queso*

*Lucille's Bean Patties*

*Red Beans and Coconut*

*Vegetarian Red Bean Lasagne*

*Bean Enchiladas*

*Red and White Chili*

*B & B*

*Bean and Cornbread Pie*

*Adzukis with Stir-Fry Vegetables and Pasta*

*Peasant Beans*

*Island Baked Beans*

*Red Beans and Rice*

*Orzo and Beans*

*Holupki*

## DESSERTS

*Pinto Bean Carrot Cake*

*Southern Peach and Walnut Bread*

*Apple Spice Pudding*

*Peanut Butter Cookies*

*Pumpkin Pecan Cranberry Bean Bread*

# Appetizers

## STUFFED MUSHROOMS

15 MUSHROOMS

These tasty morsels are nothing short of outrageous. One of the most fun parts of the great bean adventure is the disbelief factor of family and friends when something is just *too good* to be made from *beans*.

---

15 large white stuffing mushrooms

2 cups small red beans, drained and rinsed

2 tablespoons water

1 egg

3 tablespoons extra virgin olive oil

2 tablespoons butter

1 tablespoon minced garlic

1 small onion, finely diced

1 tablespoon dried parsley

3 tablespoons Italian flavored bread crumbs

4–5 shakes Tabasco sauce

¼–½ cup grated Parmesan cheese (maybe a little more, as you will use a teaspoon per mushroom)

1 cup dry white wine

---

Preheat oven to 375° F.

Wash and remove stems from mushrooms. Place the caps in a baking dish. Place the stems in a food processor and process until finely chopped. Remove to a small bowl.

Place beans in the food processor with 2 tablespoons of water and process until smooth. Add the egg to the beans and blend until light and fluffy. Transfer to a medium-size bowl.

In a medium skillet, heat the olive oil and butter. Add the garlic, onion, chopped mushroom stems, and parsley. Sauté until onions and mushrooms are soft, about 5 minutes. Remove from heat and stir in the flavored breadcrumbs.

Add the mushroom mixture to the bean and egg mixture and stir until well blended. Add Tabasco sauce and stir again.

Generously fill each mushroom cap with the filling. Top each mushroom with grated Parmesan cheese.

Pour the white wine into the bottom of the pan around the stuffed mushrooms.

Bake for 30 to 35 minutes until tops are golden brown and mushrooms are soft.

Garnish with fresh parsley, serve immediately, and watch them vanish.

*Per serving:* calories 147, calories from fat 89, total fat 10 g, cholesterol 40 mg, carbohydrates 7 g, fiber 2 g, protein 6 g

# CURRIED CITRUS DIP

4 TO 6 SERVINGS

This delicious sweet and spicy dip is an absolutely beautiful pumpkiny yellow color. It serves well with either wheat crackers or large tortilla chips. This one will certainly stand out, not only because of the vibrant color, but because its unusual combination of flavors is not the usual party-dip style.

1 onion, quartered

2 cups cooked adzuki or small red beans, drained and rinsed

4 carrots, plus 1 extra for garnish

grated zest and juice of 2 oranges

1 tablespoon hot curry powder or paste

⅔ cup plain yogurt

handful fresh basil leaves

2 tablespoons fresh lemon juice

2–3 shakes Tabasco sauce

Sea salt and fresh ground pepper to taste

Place the onion quarters in a food processor and process until finely chopped. Transfer to a small saucepan.

Place beans into the food processor and blend until almost smooth but still with some texture. Transfer to a mixing bowl.

Peel and grate the carrots. Place the carrots, orange zest, juice, and curry powder into the saucepan with the chopped onions. Bring to a boil and simmer for about 10 minutes, covered, until soft.

Process this cooked mixture in a blender or food processor until smooth and let cool completely.

Stir the carrot mixture into the beans and add the yogurt, mixing well.

Chop the basil leaves into largish pieces and mix them in.

Add the lemon juice and Tabasco and season with salt and pepper.

Garnish with a basil sprig and grated carrot.

Beautiful!

*Per serving:* calories 178, calories from fat 8, total fat 1 g, cholesterol 2 mg, carbohydrates 36 g, fiber 10 g, protein 9 g

# DEAN'S BEANS

6 SERVINGS

Dean has sailed around the world single-handedly. I'm sure that his beans were as much a hit at an anchorage in Greece as they were at our marina, where no cocktail party or pot luck dinner was complete without Dean or Dean's Beans. By the way, this could be made with one hand on the helm in ten-foot seas, so it should be no problem in your kitchen.

2 16-ounce cans refried beans (Dean prefers Old El Paso)

4 ounces hot salsa

1 tablespoon minced or dried garlic

red chili powder (Dean uses Chimayo Red Chili), anywhere from 1 pinch to 2 tablespoons (if you have a tough group)

Mix the above ingredients together well. Let sit for an hour to allow flavors to blend.

Serve with crackers or big corn chips.

What adds to the flavor of this dip is listening to Dean's stories, but it's almost as good without.

*Per serving:* calories 88, calories from fat 10, total fat 1 g, cholesterol 7 mg, carbohydrates 15 g, fiber 5 g, protein 5 g

# RED BEAN PÂTÉ

8 SERVINGS

The exceptional toasted flavor of the walnuts and the perfect blend of fresh herbs combine to create an extraordinarily rich pâté of, yes, beans.

1 cup walnuts

3 cups cooked kidney beans, drained and rinsed

5 tablespoons unsalted butter, softened

½ teaspoon garlic, minced

1 tablespoon chopped fresh dill

1 tablespoon chopped fresh basil

1 tablespoon chopped fresh parsley

kosher salt and fresh ground black pepper to taste

pita wedges, toasted

2 large (about fist-size) thinly sliced fresh mozzarella balls

fresh basil leaves for garnish

olive oil and garlic spray

Preheat oven to 350° F.

Put the walnuts in a pie plate and spread out to a single layer. Bake in a preheated oven for about 7 minutes or until the nuts are lightly toasted. Remove from oven and let cool completely.

Put the walnuts, beans, butter, and garlic into a food processor and purée until smooth. Add the dill, basil, parsley, salt, and pepper. Process again just until blended.

Transfer the pâté onto a long sheet of plastic wrap and shape into an oblong 12 x 2-inch shape. Wrap tightly and refrigerate for at least 2 hours. For serving, remove wrap and slice the pâté into slices about ½ inch thick.

Serve with toasted pita wedges (recipe below) and thin slices of the fresh mozzarella, garnished with leaves of fresh basil.

## Pita Wedges

Preheat oven to 450° F.

Cut a pita bread into 8 wedges. Spray both sides with an olive oil and garlic spray. Layer the wedges onto a cookie sheet and bake for 5 to 7 minutes or until golden and crispy.

*Per serving:* calories 248, calories from fat 148, total fat 17 g, cholesterol 19 mg, carbohydrates 18 g, fiber 6 g, protein 8 g

# STUFFED CELERY

6 SERVINGS

This is a delicious filling for celery that will be used on a crudités platter. It is also an excellent condiment for sandwiches, using it like mayonnaise.

---

1 cup cooked pinto beans

1 cup whipped cream cheese

1 teaspoon soy sauce or tamari

¼ teaspoon coriander

¼ teaspoon cumin powder

¼ teaspoon paprika

dash cayenne pepper

1 clove garlic, finely minced

---

Mash the beans well and stir together the remaining ingredients. Chill for an hour to allow flavors to blend.

Cut celery stalks into 3-inch sections, and fill with the spread.

Dust with a little extra paprika.

*Per serving:* calories 171, calories from fat 121, total fat 14 g, cholesterol 42 mg, carbohydrates 7 g, fiber 2 g, protein 5 g

# Salads, Soups & Sides

## BULGUR AND RED BEAN SALAD

6 SERVINGS

This appetizing and beautiful salad can easily be served as a main course for lunch.

2 cups bulgur

1 cup frozen baby peas

1 cup cooked small red beans, drained and rinsed

1 cup grape tomatoes, cut in half

1 medium red onion, chopped

1 yellow bell pepper, seeded and chopped

1 cup raw snow peas, cut in half

1 bunch watercress

2 tablespoons chopped fresh parsley

1 tablespoon chopped fresh basil

2 teaspoons chopped fresh thyme (or 1 teaspoon dried)

salt and pepper to taste

Soak and cook the bulgur according to the package directions. Drain and put into a large serving bowl.

Meanwhile, cook the peas in boiling water for 3 minutes. Drain and add to the cooked bulgur along with the red beans.

Add the tomatoes, onion, pepper, snow peas, and watercress to the bulgur mixture. Toss well. Add the parsley, basil, thyme, and dressing to taste. Season with salt and pepper. Toss and serve immediately.

### Dressing

1 small clove garlic, crushed

½ cup red wine vinegar

1 teaspoon Dijon mustard

1 dash Worcestershire sauce

1 cup extra virgin olive oil

salt and pepper to taste

Put all ingredients into a jar with a tight-fitting lid and shake until smooth.

Serve this with hot whole-wheat bread and maybe a little chutney on the side for a dash of extra flavor (not that it's needed). Sometimes sensory overload is a good thing.

*Per serving:* calories 454, calories from fat 323, total fat 37 g, cholesterol 0 mg, carbohydrates 28 g, fiber 7 g, protein 7 g

# RED AND GREEN BEAN SALAD

6 SERVINGS

A simple side dish with a wine-and-garlic combination that gives this salad a taste of France.

---

1 tablespoon olive oil

3 tablespoons butter

1 large onion, finely chopped

2 tablespoons finely minced garlic

4 fresh tomatoes, peeled and chopped

2 cups cooked small red beans, drained and rinsed

1 pound fresh green beans, trimmed and cut in half

⅔ cup white wine

⅔ cup chicken broth (or vegetable broth)

¼ cup chopped fresh parsley

salt and pepper to taste

---

Heat the olive oil and butter in a large skillet. Sauté the onion and garlic for 2 to 3 minutes or until soft.

Add the chopped tomatoes to the onion mixture and cook over low heat until tomatoes are soft.

Stir the red beans into the skillet and add the green beans, wine, and broth. Cover and simmer for 8 to 10 minutes.

Turn up the heat to reduce the liquid; then stir in the parsley.

Season with salt and pepper.

*Per serving:* calories 224, calories from fat 78, total fat 9 g, cholesterol 16 mg, carbohydrates 26 g, fiber 8 g, protein 8 g

# RED BEAN AND PICKLE SALAD

5 SERVINGS

This lemony, picniky, summery salad is an exquisite blend of flavors. It looks beautiful served on a brightly colored or hand-painted platter.

1½ cups dried kidney beans

2 sprigs fresh thyme

1 bay leaf

1 large onion, cut in half

2 tablespoons finely minced garlic

2 teaspoons cumin seeds, crushed

4 scallions, finely chopped (both white and green parts)

¼ cup chopped fresh parsley

juice of ½ lemon

¼ cup light olive oil

4 hard boiled eggs, chopped

3 large sweet pickles, chopped

kosher salt and fresh ground black pepper to taste

Soak the kidney beans in water to cover overnight. Drain and rinse and transfer to a large saucepan. Cover with fresh water, bring to a boil, and boil for 10 minutes.

Reduce the heat, add the thyme, bay leaf, and halved onion. Simmer for 90 minutes or until the beans are tender.

Drain the beans and discard the bay leaf and the halved onion.

In a small bowl, combine the garlic, cumin, scallions, parsley, lemon juice, and olive oil. Season with the salt and pepper. Pour over the beans and toss gently to mix. Stir in the chopped eggs and pickles.

This salad can be served warm or cold. If you are serving it chilled, wait until serving time to stir in the eggs and pickles.

*Per serving:* calories 270, calories from fat 52, total fat 6 g, cholesterol 193 mg, carbohydrates 37 g, fiber 11 g, protein 19 g

# KIDNEY BEAN SALAD (a.k.a. Three-Bean Salad)

4 TO 6 SERVINGS

I cannot let this classic recipe disappear or get lost in the maze of new and improved recipes that appear every day. This one is every picnic I have ever gone to in my youth. I know you remember this.

½ pound green beans, trimmed and cut in half

½ pound yellow beans, trimmed and cut in half

1 15.5-ounce can kidney beans, drained and rinsed

1 14-ounce can chick peas, drained and rinsed

1 medium red onion, chopped

2 stalks celery, sliced into ¼-inch pieces

½ cup sugar or Splenda

⅓ cup red wine vinegar

⅓ cup cider vinegar

2 tablespoons olive oil

pinch of oregano

1 teaspoon minced garlic

Blanch (drop into boiling water) the green and yellow beans for 2 minutes. Rinse under cold water to stop cooking. Drain well.

Mix all of the above, tossing gently to mix well. Refrigerate for at least 2 hours to overnight. Have a picnic!

*Per serving:* calories 235, calories from fat 46, total fat 5 g, cholesterol 0 mg, carbohydrates 42 g, fiber 8 g, protein 7 g

# SOUTHWEST THREE-BEAN SALAD

6 SERVINGS

This recipe gives the three-bean a new look and taste.

---

½ pound green beans, trimmed and cut in half

1 15-ounce can yellow hominy, drained and rinsed

1 15-ounce can kidney beans, drained and rinsed

1 cup cooked pinto beans, drained and rinsed

3 large tomatoes, chopped

1 large red onion, chopped

1 cup chopped fresh cilantro

juice of 1 lime

2 tablespoons canola oil

2 teaspoons chili powder

2 teaspoons ground cumin

salt and pepper to taste

---

Blanch (drop into boiling water) the green beans for 2 minutes. Rinse under cold water to stop cooking. Drain well.

Combine all ingredients; cover and chill for at least 3 hours.

*Per serving:* calories 161, calories from fat 50, total fat 6 g, cholesterol 0 mg, carbohydrates 23 g, fiber 6 g, protein 6 g

# RED POTATO SALAD

6 SERVINGS

A potato salad like no other.

---

½ cup mayonnaise

1 cup sour cream

1 teaspoon minced garlic

½ teaspoon sugar or sweetener

½ teaspoon dried dill

4 tablespoons finely chopped fresh parsley (divided use)

sea salt and fresh ground pepper to taste

2 cups baby red potatoes, cooked and quartered

2 cups cooked pinto beans, drained and rinsed

1 medium cucumber, peeled and diced

1 small red onion, chopped

---

Mix mayonnaise, sour cream, garlic, sugar, dill, 3 tablespoons of the parsley, salt, and pepper.

In a large bowl, combine the potatoes, beans, cucumber, and red onion. Add the mayonnaise mixture and gently fold in until well mixed. Top with the extra chopped parsley and cover with plastic wrap. Chill for at least 2 hours.

*Per serving:* calories 119, calories from fat 7, total fat 1 g, cholesterol 0 mg, carbohydrates 24 g, fiber 5 g, protein 5 g

# WHITE TUNA AND KIDNEY BEANS

4 SERVINGS

This salad is a very quick put-together. You have the option of using low-fat mayonnaise and fat-free yogurt to make it a nutritionally well-rounded and low-calorie lunch.

---

2 cups cooked kidney beans, drained and rinsed

1 6.5-ounce can water-packed solid white tuna

¾ cup chopped celery

¼ cup chopped green pepper

¼ cup chopped red pepper

3 tablespoons mayonnaise

2 tablespoons plain yogurt

3 tablespoons pickle relish

fresh ground black pepper

---

Mix together the beans, tuna, celery, and peppers. In a small bowl, combine the mayonnaise, yogurt, and relish. Add to the bean and tuna mixture and gently stir.

Add black pepper to taste.

Serve this on top of a romaine or curly lettuce with rye crisps on the side.

*Per serving:* calories 457, calories from fat 54, total fat 6 g, cholesterol 22 mg, carbohydrates 68 g, fiber 16 g, protein 35 g

# CONFETTI SALAD

4 TO 6 SERVINGS

This salad is a summery burst of colors and flavors, and it's good any time of the year.

---

1 15.5-ounce can small red beans, drained and rinsed

1 11-ounce can white corn (or 2 ears fresh corn, lightly steamed, cooled, and cut from cob)

½ orange bell pepper, diced

3 scallions, diced (both green and white parts)

1 4-ounce can chopped green chilies

2 tablespoons olive oil

juice of ½ fresh lime

¼ cup tomato sauce

2 teaspoons fresh chopped parsley

2 teaspoons fresh chopped cilantro

fresh ground black pepper to taste

---

Toss all the ingredients gently to mix well and refrigerate for at least 2 hours for the flavors to develop.

Serve on a clear glass plate if possible with a bit of greenery around the edges.

*Per serving:* calories 202, calories from fat 65, total fat 7 g, cholesterol 0 mg, carbohydrates 28 g, fiber 9 g, protein 8 g

# BEET AND BEAN BORSCHT

6 TO 8 SERVINGS

Classic borscht is an amazingly healthful dish, but with the addition of beans you not only get more body, texture, and taste, but soaring nutrition as well.

---

3 large beets

8 cups clear beef broth (or a rich vegetable broth)

1 large onion, chopped

3 cups shredded green cabbage

1½ cups cooked red kidney beans or small red beans, drained and rinsed

1 tablespoon butter

4 teaspoons lemon juice

kosher salt and fresh ground black pepper to taste

sour cream (for topping)

---

Wash and peel the beets. Grate them coarsely. (Rubber gloves are usually a good idea, unless you don't mind burgundy-colored hands for a day or two.)

Bring broth to a boil in a large soup pan. Add chopped onion and beets to the boiling broth. Cook for 15 to 20 minutes. Add cabbage and the beans. Cook for another 10 minutes. Add butter, lemon juice, salt, and pepper.

Serve in soup bowls with a dollop of sour cream and fresh chopped parsley on top.

*Per serving:* calories 195, calories from fat 24, total fat 3 g, cholesterol 5 mg, carbohydrates 33 g, fiber 8 g, protein 12 g

# ADZUKI SOUP

4 SERVINGS

There's a touch of the Orient in this comforting, high-protein soup.

---

4 cups vegetable broth (or chicken broth)

3 cups cooked adzuki beans, drained and rinsed

2 teaspoons peanut oil

4 carrots, cut diagonally into thin slices

¼ cup white miso

4 scallions, thinly sliced (both green and white parts)

black pepper to taste

---

In a large saucepan, bring broth to a boil. Add beans and simmer for 15 minutes, stirring occasionally.

In a wok or heavy skillet, heat oil over a moderately high heat and stir-fry carrots until they are crisply tender, about 2 to 3 minutes. Stir carrots into the soup.

In a small bowl, combine miso and 1 cup of the hot broth, stirring until the miso is dissolved and smooth. Pour back into soup and stir again. Add in the scallions and black pepper.

*Per serving:* calories 394, calories from fat 84, total fat 10 g, cholesterol 0 mg, carbohydrates 58 g, fiber 16 g, protein 21 g

# RED BEAN SOUP

6 SERVINGS

A chilly night dinner that could easily and deliciously be passed on a day or two to become a chilly afternoon lunch. Add a little green salad either way.

---

2 cups dried red beans (soaked for 4 hours in water to cover)

4 tablespoons extra virgin olive oil

1 large yellow onion, chopped

3 carrots, peeled and chopped

3 stalks celery, thinly sliced

2 tablespoons minced garlic

¼ cup finely chopped fresh parsley (divided use)

4 tablespoons finely chopped fresh basil (divided use)

2 cups chicken broth (or vegetable broth)

2+ cups water

1 tablespoon chopped fresh sage

1 bay leaf

2 pounds plum tomatoes, chopped

sea salt and fresh ground pepper to taste

---

Drain and rinse the soaked beans.

Heat oil in a large soup pot over medium heat. Add onion, carrots, and celery. Cook until the vegetables are just soft, about 10 minutes. Add garlic and 1 tablespoon each of the parsley and basil. Stir and cook for another 5 minutes.

Add the broth, water, beans, sage, and bay leaf. Simmer over medium-low heat for 90 minutes or until beans are tender. Water should cover beans, so add water if necessary as the soup cooks.

Add tomatoes and remaining parsley and basil. Cook for another 45 minutes. Season with salt and pepper to taste.

*Per serving:* calories 155, calories from fat 89, total fat 10 g, cholesterol 0 mg, carbohydrates 14 g, fiber 4 g, protein 4 g

# THREE CHILI AND BEAN SOUP

6 TO 8 SERVINGS

A deeply flavored soup that is unbelievably simple to make.

---

1 pound pinto beans, sorted and washed

3 medium onions, coarsely chopped

3 cloves garlic, minced

1 tablespoon ground cumin

1 tablespoon coriander

1 teaspoon dried oregano

½ teaspoon cinnamon

4 quarts water

2 jalapeño peppers, seeded and chopped

4 pasilla chilies, stemmed, seeded, and chopped

3 New Mexico chilies, stemmed, seeded, and chopped

2 canned chipotle chilies, stemmed

7 cups chicken broth (or vegetable broth)

½ cup chopped fresh cilantro (plus extra for garnish)

salt and pepper to taste

1 cup sour cream (for garnish)

Soak beans in water to cover for 24 hours, changing water at least twice. Drain and rinse beans and place in a 12-quart pot along with onions, garlic, cumin, coriander, oregano, cinnamon, water, jalapeños, and chilies. Bring to a boil over high heat. Reduce heat to moderate and simmer 1 to 1½ hours, until beans are tender. Remove from heat. Cool to room temperature.

Add the broth and cilantro; mix well. In a blender or food processor, purée soup in batches until smooth. Return to pot and bring to boil over high heat. Reduce heat and simmer 20 to 25 minutes, stirring occasionally until soup is thickened. Season with salt and pepper.

Serve in large bowls with a dollop of sour cream and extra chopped cilantro on top.

Serve alongside a basket of warm corn tortillas and a pitcher of fresh sangria to cool the tongue.

*Per serving:* calories 306, calories from fat 31, total fat 4 g, cholesterol 0 mg, carbohydrates 51 g, fiber 13 g, protein 19 g

# BARBECUE CALICO BEANS

8 SERVINGS

Here's an old-time picnic potluck dish. The extra piquant flavor in this recipe brings the richness of all the other ingredients together nicely.

## Sauce

4 tablespoons butter

⅓ cup minced onion

1 clove garlic, minced

4 tablespoons olive oil

½ cup wine vinegar

½ cup chili sauce

½ cup tomato purée

¼ cup water

3 tablespoons Worcestershire sauce

⅛ teaspoon thyme

⅛ teaspoon oregano

⅛ teaspoon tarragon

In a saucepan, melt butter; add onion and garlic. Sauté for 2 minutes until onion is straw-colored.

Add the remaining ingredients and simmer over low heat for 40 minutes.

## Beans

2 15.5-ounce cans kidney beans, drained and rinsed

2 15.5-ounce cans pinto beans, drained and rinsed

2 15.5-ounce cans lima beans, drained and rinsed

Preheat oven to 350° F.

Combine the drained beans into a large baking casserole. Pour the barbecue sauce over the beans. Bake 30 to 40 minutes until the beans are sizzling hot. Serve right from the casserole.

Place this next to the cold watermelon on the picnic table and watch them both disappear.

*Per serving:* calories 329, calories from fat 119, total fat 14 g, cholesterol 16 mg, carbohydrates 41 g, fiber 14 g, protein 13 g

# Main Dishes

. . . . . . . . . . . . . . . . . . . . . . . . . . . . . . . . . . . . .

## CHUCK'S RESURRECTED RED BEANS

4 TO 6 SERVINGS

My husband, Chuck, is the inspiration for this book. Cutting red meat out of his diet and having his "daily bean" helped him keep his blood sugar under control without insulin injections. Now Chuck is creating his own bean fantasies. He wings this very easy but tasty recipe, changing quantities and even ingredients, adding extra hot stuff as he goes. You can wing this, too. Have fun and be brave: All is forgiven with the hot pepper.

2 tablespoons olive oil

2 cloves garlic, crushed

2 green peppers, chopped

1 large yellow onion, chopped

3 tablespoons Recaito

4 15.5-ounce cans red beans, drained and rinsed

2 28-ounce cans crushed tomatoes

2 8-ounce cans tomato sauce

crushed red pepper flakes to taste

## Optional Toppings

chopped scallions

shredded Monterey jack and cheddar cheese

sour cream

Heat olive oil over medium heat in a large saucepan. Add garlic, green peppers, and onions, cooking until soft but not brown. Adding the rest of the ingredients, stir and bring to a boil. Turn down heat and simmer, uncovered for 20 to 25 minutes, stirring occasionally.

Serve in large warmed bowls with whatever toppings you choose.

Add an ice cold beer along with crusty bread and crisp green salad . . . and bring on the football!!

*Per serving:* calories 408, calories from fat 55, total fat 6 g, cholesterol 0 mg, carbohydrates 72 g, protein 21 g, fiber 26 g

. . . .
150

# RATATOUILLE

4 SERVINGS

This classic winter vegetable side dish is made hearty enough for a lunch main course with the tasty addition of red beans.

2 large eggplants, chopped into 1-inch squares

3 large zucchinis, chopped into 1-inch squares

⅔ cup extra virgin olive oil

2 large onions, chopped

2 large cloves garlic, finely chopped

1 large red pepper, seeded and chopped

1 large yellow pepper, seeded and chopped

2 cups cooked red beans, drained and rinsed

2 sprigs fresh thyme

1 teaspoon coriander seeds, crushed

3 large tomatoes, chopped

salt and pepper to taste

¼ cup finely chopped fresh basil

¼ cup finely chopped fresh parsley

basil leaves for garnish

dark bread, cut into large hunks

Combine the eggplant and zucchini in a large colander and sprinkle with salt. Weigh them down with a large plate to extract the extra fluids. Let sit for about 45 minutes.

Heat the olive oil in a large saucepan. Add the onions and cook over low heat for 6 to 7 minutes, until just softened. Add the garlic.

Rinse and pat dry the eggplant and zucchini. Add to the saucepan with the onions and garlic. Add the peppers and increase heat. Sauté until the peppers are just turning brown. Add the beans, thyme, and coriander; stir and cover pan. Cook gently for 40 minutes. Add the chopped tomatoes, salt, and pepper. Cook for another 10 minutes. Stir in the basil and parsley.

Let cool and serve either warm or chilled, garnished with basil leaves and big hunks of a dark bread.

*Per serving:* calories 343, calories from fat 219, total fat 25 g, cholesterol 0 mg, carbohydrates 26 g, fiber 9 g, protein 7 g

# FRIJOLES CON CHILES Y QUESO

8 SERVINGS

This is a speedy put-together for a hungry group. Send someone out for some Coronas while this is in the oven.

---

3 15.5-ounce cans small red beans, drained and rinsed (divided use)

½ teaspoon basil

¼ teaspoon oregano

½ teaspoon garlic powder

3 4-ounce cans diced mild green chilies (divided use)

2 cups grated Monterey Jack cheese (divided use)

1 cup sour cream

1½–2 cups chicken broth (or vegetable broth)

---

Preheat oven to 325° F.

Mix beans, basil, oregano, and garlic powder.

Spread half the beans in a 3-quart oven casserole. Sprinkle with half the chopped green chilies. Top with half of the grated cheese. Add another layer of beans and top with the remaining chilies and cheese.

Stir the broth into the sour cream and mix until smooth. Pour liquid over the beans in the casserole. The cream should almost cover the beans.

Bake uncovered for 30 to 45 minutes or until bubbling.

Serve with warm tortillas for dipping. Have fresh sliced limes on hand for taste, color, and the Coronas.

*Per serving:* calories 334, calories from fat 128, total fat 15, cholesterol 41 mg, carbohydrates 31 g, fiber 12 g, protein 20 g

# LUCILLE'S BEAN PATTIES

4 PATTIES

My sister Lucille came up with this great alternative to hamburgers. The little Southwestern twang makes these totally satisfying for lunch or dinner.

---

1 15.5-ounce can pinto beans, drained and rinsed

½ small onion, chopped

1 4-ounce can chopped green chilies, drained

4 ounces sharp cheddar cheese, shredded

¼ teaspoon chili powder

pinch of salt

1 egg, lightly beaten

½ cup corn meal (divided use)

2 tablespoons butter, melted

Tabasco to taste

---

Preheat oven to 425° F and grease a baking sheet.

Mix beans, onion, chilies, cheddar cheese, chili powder, salt, egg, and ⅓ cup of the corn meal.

Form into 4 patties and coat with the remaining cornmeal. Place on the prepared baking sheet, drizzle with the melted butter, and sprinkle each patty with Tabasco to taste.

Bake 20 minutes, turning only once at 10 minutes.

These are very tasty as is or served on a whole-wheat roll with a slice of tomato and a slice of red onion.

*Per serving:* calories 302, calories from fat 125, total fat 14 g, cholesterol 94 mg, carbohydrates 31 g, fiber 7 g, protein 13 g

# RED BEANS AND COCONUT

6 SERVINGS

If you have a palm tree in your yard and the Caribbean Sea at your stoop, just open the door and let the salt breeze help flavor this tropical stew-like dish. If not, just pretend and add a bit more salt yourself.

---

1 pound pink beans, rinsed and soaked overnight

2 cloves garlic, minced

1 large onion, chopped

1 tomato, diced

2 cups peeled, cubed Caribbean pumpkin (calabaza) (or substitute acorn squash)

salt and pepper to taste

1½ cups unsweetened coconut cream

---

Drain and rinse beans. Cover with fresh water, about 1 inch over the beans, in a large pot. Bring to a boil, reduce heat, and simmer until beans are tender, 1½ to 2 hours. If the water evaporates, add more boiling water.

Add the garlic, onion, tomato, and pumpkin. Cook until they are tender. Remove some of the pumpkin and beans and mash in a separate bowl. Return to the pot to thicken. Add salt and pepper to taste. Finally, add the coconut cream and cook for 10 minutes.

Complete the picture with fried plantains and rice.

*Per serving:* calories 342, calories from fat 120, total fat 14 g, cholesterol 0 mg, carbohydrates 46 g, fiber 13 g, protein 12 g

# VEGETARIAN RED BEAN LASAGNA

10 TO 12 SERVINGS

This lasagna is just as cheesy, saucy, and satisfying as any classic Italian lasagna. And thanks to the red beans, you'll never miss the ground beef.

2 tablespoons olive oil

1 large onion, chopped

1 medium carrot, chopped

2 cloves garlic, minced

2 cups tomatoes, chopped

2 cups cooked red beans, rinsed and drained

¼ cup fresh chopped parsley

1 teaspoon dried oregano

salt to taste

1 teaspoon dried basil

1 egg, beaten

2 cups ricotta cheese

½ cup Parmesan cheese

2 cups shredded mozzarella cheese

1 box lasagna noodles

3–3½ cups spaghetti sauce

Preheat oven to 375° F.

In a large saucepan, heat olive oil, and sauté onion, carrot, and garlic for 2 to 3 minutes. Add tomatoes, beans, parsley, oregano, basil, and salt. Bring to a boil, reduce heat, and simmer for about 15 minutes.

In a small bowl, combine the beaten egg with the ricotta, ¼ cup of the Parmesan, and half of the mozzarella .

Cook lasagna noodles as directed on box.

In a 13 x 9 x 2-inch baking dish, spread about ½ cup spaghetti sauce. Place one layer of lasagna noodles across the bottom of the dish. Distribute a third of the ricotta mixture evenly over the noodles. Top with a third of the vegetable and bean mixture. Spread about ¾ cup of sauce over the top of the bean mixture. Top with another layer of lasagna noodles. Repeat the layering steps twice more, finishing with a layer of noodles. Top with sauce and the remaining cup of mozzarella and ¼ cup Parmesan.

Cover with aluminum foil and bake for 30 minutes. Remove foil and bake for another 10 to 15 minutes until mozzarella and Parmesan are bubbling.

Let stand for 5 minutes before cutting.

Serve with all the classic trimmings: salad, garlic bread, Chianti, cannolis, espresso, and anisette. Buon apetito!

*Per serving:* calories 435, calories from fat 101, total fat 11 g, cholesterol 59 mg, carbohydrates 58 g, fiber 6 g, protein 26 g

# BEAN ENCHILADAS

4 SERVINGS

A spicy, healthy entrée for a Mexican-night dinner or buffet. These enchiladas contain two types of beans, the soybeans adding even more protein and flavor.

1 cup cooked kidney or pinto beans

1 cup cooked soybeans

1 medium onion, chopped

2 cloves garlic, minced

1 tablespoon fresh, finely chopped cilantro

1 tablespoon chili powder

1 teaspoon ground cumin

2 teaspoons soy sauce

1 tablespoon lemon juice

8 corn tortillas

½ cup shredded sharp cheddar cheese

½ cup shredded Monterey Jack cheese

3 cups enchilada sauce (feel free to use a store-bought sauce to make this an even easier production)

Preheat the oven to 350° F.

Mash or purée beans in a food processor or blender until smooth. In a small saucepan, steam-cook onions in a small amount of water, stirring until they begin to brown.

Add garlic, cilantro, chili powder, cumin, soy sauce, lemon juice, and the bean purée to the onions. Stir over low heat until heated through and mixed well.

## Enchilada Sauce

1 tablespoon olive oil

1 tablespoon minced garlic

1 tablespoon minced onion

1 14-ounce can tomato sauce

1½ cups water

1 4-ounce can chopped green chilies

1 tablespoon tomato paste

3 tablespoons chili powder

½ teaspoon ground cumin

salt and pepper to taste

1 teaspoon dried parsley

Heat the olive oil in a saucepan and add garlic and onion. Sauté briefly, 1 to 2 minutes. Add the rest of the ingredients to the saucepan and bring to a boil. Reduce heat and simmer for 15 to 20 minutes.

Soften corn tortillas by placing each one briefly into a heated, small, oiled skillet, turning once.

Place about ⅓ cup of the bean mixture on each tortilla and roll up. Place seam-side-down in a casserole dish and cover with the enchilada sauce. Sprinkle with both cheeses and bake for 15 to 20 minutes until the sauce bubbles and the cheese melts.

Top with sour cream, guacamole, and chopped scallions.

*Per serving:* calories 509, calories from fat 145, total fat 17 g, cholesterol 32 mg, carbohydrates 63 g, fiber 14 g, protein 30 g

# RED AND WHITE CHILI

14 SERVINGS

A spicy, spicy blend of protein and veggies. One could devote a book entirely to chili recipes (and I'm sure someone has!). Beans lend themselves so well to this hearty favorite, I just keep slipping in different great tastes in chili with another color bean and inventive combinations of vegetables and spices.

---

¼ cup vegetable oil

¼ cup olive oil

1 cup diced celery

2 cups diced sweet onion

1 cup diced red bell pepper

1 cup diced yellow pepper

5 cloves garlic, minced

5 tablespoons chili powder

3 tablespoons ground cumin

1 tablespoon crushed red pepper

3 bay leaves

6 cups crushed tomatoes

5 cups cooked red beans, drained and rinsed

5 cups cooked white beans, drained and rinsed

2 teaspoons kosher salt

3 cups extra firm tofu, cut into ½-inch cubes

---

In a large pot, heat the oils and sauté the celery and onions until tender. Add the peppers and garlic, stirring often, until the peppers are tender.

Add the chili powder, cumin, crushed red pepper, and bay leaves; stir and cook for 5 minutes.

Add the crushed tomatoes; stir and bring to a simmer.

Add the beans and salt. Simmer for 45 minutes, stirring occasionally.

Gently fold in the cubed tofu.

Serve with whatever chili accouterments you choose.

*Per serving:* calories 453, calories from fat 86, total fat 10 g, cholesterol 0 mg, carbohydrates 71 g, fiber 20 g, protein 26 g

# B & B (Bowties and Beans)

4 TO 6 SERVINGS

The six—and only six—main ingredients combine flavor and color with extreme simplicity and shortness of preparation time to create a perfect weekday meal.

---

8 ounces bowtie pasta

2 tablespoons olive oil

6 cups baby spinach leaves

1 tablespoon garlic, minced

1 15-ounce can red kidney beans, drained and rinsed

½ cup freshly grated Romano cheese

salt and fresh ground black pepper to taste

fresh basil leaves for garnish

---

Cook the pasta according to package directions. In a large separate skillet, sauté the spinach and garlic in the olive oil until spinach is wilted.

Toss the beans and bowties with the spinach and cheese. Season with the salt and pepper.

Garnish with some big beautiful fresh basil leaves and serve with a fresh tomato and mozzarella salad.

*Per serving:* calories 297, calories from fat 71, total fat 8 g, cholesterol 7 mg, carbohydrates 43 g, fiber 7 g, protein 14 g

# BEAN AND CORNBREAD PIE

4 SERVINGS

A meal unto itself, combining the comforting flavors of hot cornbread, cheese, and a little spice.

---

2 15.5-ounce cans kidney beans, drained and rinsed

¾ cup chopped onion

3 tablespoons vegetable oil

1 teaspoon minced garlic

2 teaspoons chili powder

salt to taste

2 tablespoons catsup

3 tablespoons water

1 cup corn kernels

½ green bell pepper, diced

¼ cup chopped parsley

½ cup diced celery

½ cup cornmeal

½ cup flour

2 teaspoons baking powder

½ cup milk

½ cup grated cheddar cheese

---

Preheat oven to 350° F. Lightly grease an 8 x 8-inch pan.

Mash one can of the kidney beans with a fork or potato masher.

Sauté the onion in 1 tablespoon of the oil in a large skillet. Add beans, both mashed and whole, along with garlic, chili powder, salt, catsup, water, corn, green pepper, parsley, and celery to the skillet. Cook over medium heat for 5 minutes, stirring occasionally to keep bean mixture from sticking.

Combine cornmeal, flour, baking powder, and a pinch of salt in a small mixing bowl. Add milk and 2 tablespoons of oil to the cornmeal mixture and stir until blended.

Spread two-thirds of the cornmeal mixture over the bottom of the prepared pan. Pour the bean mixture onto the cornmeal crust. Spread the remaining cornmeal mixture on top of the beans, into four flat circular shapes to top and define each of the portions.

Sprinkle with grated cheddar cheese and bake for 30 minutes.

Serve with tangy coleslaw for a satisfying down-home dinner.

*Per serving:* calories 563, calories from fat 315, total fat 36 g, cholesterol 46 mg, carbohydrates 48 g, fiber 13 g, protein 15 g

# ADZUKIS WITH STIR-FRY VEGETABLES AND PASTA

4 TO 6 SERVINGS

The savory flavors of this oriental dish are augmented with beans and pasta.

---

8 ounces orecchiette pasta (little hats)

1½ tablespoons peanut oil

1 large onion, quartered and thinly sliced

1 tablespoon minced fresh garlic

1 cup broccoli florets, cut into bite-sized pieces

1 cup snow peas

½ cup carrots, thinly sliced on the diagonal

2 ripe tomatoes, diced

2 cups cooked adzuki beans, drained and rinsed

2 slices of fresh ginger, cut into very thin strips

3 tablespoons dark miso

2 tablespoons cornstarch

1 cup warm water

1 teaspoon dark sesame oil (plus extra to taste)

3 scallions, chopped (both green and white parts)

---

Cook the pasta according to package directions for *al dente*. Drain and set aside in a large serving bowl.

Heat the oil in a large skillet over medium-high heat. Add onion, garlic, broccoli, snow peas, and carrots. Stir-fry until the broccoli is bright green, about 2 minutes.

Add the tomatoes, adzuki beans, and ginger. Lower heat and simmer for 10 minutes.

In a small bowl, combine the miso, cornstarch, and water, stirring until smooth. Pour into the skillet with the vegetables and add the sesame oil. Stir to mix and simmer gently until the liquid has thickened.

Pour the sauce and bean mixture over the pasta and gently fold to combine. Serve immediately. Sprinkle the top of each serving with the scallions. Use additional dark sesame oil as a condiment to drizzle over the top of each individual serving.

An ice-cold plum wine follows this down just beautifully.

*Per serving:* calories 591, calories from fat 115, total fat 13 g, cholesterol 0 mg, carbohydrates 93 g, fiber 16 g, protein 29 g

# PEASANT BEANS

8 SERVINGS

This is a hearty, rustic dish that was probably first made for a farmer's lunch in the hills of Italy. It has found its way to more sophisticated tables by sheer taste alone.

---

4–5 medium potatoes, peeled and cut into bite-sized pieces

5 Italian plum tomatoes, cut into wedges

2 large red onions, quartered and thinly sliced (divided use)

2–3 tablespoons extra virgin olive oil

1 tablespoon balsamic vinegar

salt and pepper to taste

fresh basil, chopped

olive oil (enough to cover bottom of large skillet)

3 frying peppers, seeds removed, cut into strips

3 cloves garlic, minced

3 small zucchinis, thinly sliced

2 cups cooked pinto beans, drained and rinsed

---

In salted water, boil potatoes. Drain, but reserve the liquid. Set aside and keep warm.

Toss together the plum tomatoes, 1 sliced red onion, extra virgin olive oil, vinegar, salt, and pepper. Arrange on a platter and garnish with chopped fresh basil. Set aside.

Heat enough olive oil to cover the bottom of a heavy skillet.

Add the peppers and sauté until they are nearly cooked through. Add the garlic and cook for 1 or 2 minutes. Set aside.

Sauté zucchini and remaining red onion in the same skillet, adding more olive oil if needed.

Toss the peppers and zucchini together with the beans and potatoes. Add a small amount of the warm liquid that remains from boiling the potatoes. Serve in soup bowls, topping each serving with the tomato salad.

Have long crusty loaves available for ripping and dipping. Some hearty red wine wouldn't hurt either.

*Per serving:* calories 179, calories from fat 8, total fat 1 g, cholesterol 0 mg, carbohydrates 39 g, fiber 7 g, protein 7 g

## ISLAND BAKED BEANS

10 SERVINGS

In St. Croix, as well as in the States, people have fought over who will make this to bring to the party. Suzanne Benson, living out the fantasy life of many on the island of St. Croix, is responsible for this amazing "Baked Beans goes Caribbean" dish.

---

1 15.5-ounce can pinto beans, drained and rinsed

1 15.5-ounce can kidney beans, drained and rinsed

1 15.5-ounce can black beans, drained and rinsed

1 red onion, chopped and sautéed in 1 tablespoon oil

1 8-ounce can crushed pineapple in natural juice

½ cup orange juice

¼ cup molasses

¼ cup maple syrup (real stuff only)

1 tablespoon curry powder

1 tablespoon dry mustard

1 teaspoon Chinese 5-spice or pumpkin pie spice

---

Preheat oven to 325° F.

Combine all ingredients in casserole and bake for 1 to 1½ hours.

Leftovers are almost better than the first day, if that's possible, so you might even want to double the recipe. This is also good served with a fragrant basmati rice.

*Per serving:* calories 204, calories from fat 8, total fat 1 g, cholesterol 0 mg, carbohydrates 42 g, fiber 8 g, protein 8 g

# RED BEANS AND RICE

4 SERVINGS

This is a hearty, meatless version of the New Orleans classic. The dish maintains a robust flavor and plenty of protein and nutrients despite the absence of the sausage.

1 cup white rice (I prefer basmati, just for the flavor)

1 tablespoon extra virgin olive oil

2 cloves garlic, minced

1 cup chopped red onion

½ cup chopped green bell pepper

1 teaspoon ground cumin

1 teaspoon dried thyme

¼ teaspoon ground red pepper

1 cup frozen peas, thawed

1 14.5-ounce can diced tomatoes

2 tablespoons orange juice

kernels from 2 ears of corn (or use thawed frozen corn)

1 19-ounce can red kidney beans, drained and rinsed

2 dashes Tabasco sauce

salt and pepper to taste

Cook rice according to package directions.

Heat the oil in a large skillet over medium-high heat. Add the garlic, onion, and green peppers, cooking for 1 minute. Add the cumin, thyme, red pepper, and peas and lower heat to medium.

Add tomatoes and orange juice. Cook for 10 minutes. Add the corn, kidney beans, and Tabasco sauce, cooking another 5 minutes or until beans are heated through.

Season with salt and pepper and additional Tabasco to taste.

Line each plate with shredded romaine lettuce leaves, top with the white rice and then the bean mixture, and you have a work of art. Sliced French bread with an herbed cheese spread fits in the picture nicely.

*Per serving:* calories 460, calories from fat 43, total fat 5 g, cholesterol 0 mg, carbohydrates 92 g, fiber 15 g, protein 17 g

# ORZO AND BEANS

4 SERVINGS

Low in fat, high in hearty taste!

---

8 ounces (about 1½ cups) orzo pasta

1 tablespoon olive oil

1 onion, chopped

2 cloves garlic, minced

1 teaspoon ground cumin

1 teaspoon oregano

1 teaspoon dried basil

kosher salt to taste

2 15.5-ounce cans kidney beans, drained and rinsed

1 10-ounce can diced tomatoes and green chilies

1 bay leaf

3 cups fresh baby spinach leaves

---

Follow directions on orzo package for *al dente*. Drain.

Heat oil in a large skillet over medium-high heat. Add the onion and garlic and cook for 2 to 3 minutes, stirring, until onions are softened.

Add the cumin, oregano, basil, and salt, mixing thoroughly. Add the kidney beans, tomatoes with green chilies, and the bay leaf. Bring to a boil, reduce heat and simmer for 10 minutes.

Stir in the spinach and cook until it is just wilted, about 2 minutes. Stir in the orzo and serve at once.

Cooked baby carrots as a side dish not only adds a contrasting splash of color but blends wonderfully with the flavors of the spinach, tomato, and green chilies.

*Per serving:* calories 476, calories from fat 47, total fat 5 g, cholesterol 0 mg, carbohydrates 87 g, fiber 18 g, protein 22 g

# HOLUPKI

5 SERVINGS

The every-other-Sunday dinner in my parent's home is a Polish dish traditionally made with a filling of ground meat and rice. The seasonings in this version are exactly the same, and the combination of the brown rice and beans creates the same if not more perfect protein content. (By the way, I have learned that when you are told the amount of an ingredient is the cup of your hand, it equals about ¼ cup, no matter what size hand.)

---

6 tablespoons extra virgin olive oil

3 large cloves garlic, minced

1 small onion, finely diced

2 cups cooked pink beans, drained and rinsed

1 cup brown rice cooked in one 15-ounce can chicken (or vegetable) broth and water to equal 2½ cups of liquid

¼ cup parsley

3 tablespoons finely chopped fresh basil (or 1½ tablespoons dried basil)

1 egg, lightly beaten

salt and pepper to taste

1 medium head cabbage

tomato sauce

---

Preheat oven to 325° F.

In a medium skillet, heat the olive oil and sauté the garlic, onion, and pink beans until the onion is just soft.

In a large bowl, combine the cooked rice, the sautéed bean mixture, parsley, basil, egg, salt, and pepper. Stir to mix.

In a large soup pot, bring enough water to boil to completely cover the head of cabbage.

Core the cabbage with a sharp knife and lower the whole cabbage into the boiling water. With a long fork, peel off the whole leaves of cabbage as they come loose in the hot water and place into a colander.

Trim the spines of each leaf with a paring knife, being careful not to cut the leaf entirely in half.

Place ¼ to ½ cup of the rice filling in each cabbage leaf. Tuck in the ends as you roll the cabbage around the filling.

Cover the bottom of a 9 x 12-inch baking dish with tomato sauce. Arrange the cabbage rolls in the dish and pour tomato sauce over to cover.

Bake in a preheated oven for 90 minutes.

*Per serving:* calories 463, calories from fat 169, total fat 19 g, cholesterol 49 mg, carbohydrates 63 g, fiber 9 g, protein 14 g

# Desserts

## PINTO BEAN CARROT CAKE

20 PIECES

At 3 grams per piece, the fiber content alone speaks volumes for the healthfulness of this cake. An extremely moist and rich cake, it won't last long if left on the kitchen counter at the mercy of wandering nibblers who haven't a clue that this very tasty morsel is so good for them.

---

1 cup brown sugar (or 1 cup Splenda)

¼ cup butter

1 egg

2 cups cooked pinto beans, mashed

1 cup flour

1 teaspoon baking soda

2 teaspoons cinnamon

½ teaspoon cloves

½ teaspoon allspice

1 tablespoon vanilla

½ cup chopped walnuts

1 cup raisins

3 cups shredded carrots

---

Preheat oven to 375° F.

Cream the sugar and butter. Add the egg and mashed bean; mix well. Add flour, baking soda, cinnamon, cloves, and allspice; mix well. Add vanilla, walnuts, raisins, carrots, and mix well again.

Pour batter into a 9 x 13-inch greased pan.

Bake for 35 to 45 minutes or until toothpick inserted in center comes out clean. Top with frosting if desired (see below)—but it's just as good without it. Feel free to use your own favorite cream cheese frosting instead of this version.

## Tofu "cream cheese" frosting

---

1 pound tofu

¼ cup maple syrup or rice syrup

¼ cup tahini (sesame butter)

¼ teaspoon orange zest

---

Whip in a food processor until smooth and creamy. Make sure the cake is absolutely cool before you add frosting.

*Per piece (without frosting):* calories 227, calories from fat 67, total fat 8 g, cholesterol 19 mg, carbohydrates 33 g, fiber 3 g, protein 9 g

# SOUTHERN PEACH AND WALNUT BREAD

16 SLICES

This very moist cakelike bread slices beautifully for a dessert platter. A nice warm slice with a little swirl of cream cheese is heavenly.

1 15.5-ounce can small red beans, drained and rinsed

2 tablespoons water

3 cups flour

2 teaspoons baking powder

¼ teaspoon salt

2 teaspoons cinnamon

3 teaspoons vanilla

1 cup buttermilk

¾ cup canola oil

1 cup brown sugar

4 eggs

6 ounces dried peaches, diced small

1 cup finely chopped walnuts

Preheat oven to 350° F. Grease two 9-inch loaf pans.

Purée the beans with 2 tablespoons of water in a food processor until very smooth.

Whisk together the flour, baking powder, salt, and cinnamon in a medium bowl.

Add the vanilla and puréed beans to the buttermilk and mix until smooth and blended.

In a large bowl, beat oil and brown sugar. Add eggs one at a time, beating after each addition. Mix in the flour mixture, alternating with the buttermilk and bean mixture and stirring well between each addition.

Fold in the peaches and walnuts.

Divide batter between 2 loaf pans and place in preheated oven. Bake for 35 to 40 minutes or until a knife inserted in the center of a loaf comes out clean.

*Per slice:* calories 472, calories from fat 152, total fat 17 g, cholesterol 62 mg, carbohydrates 74 g, fiber 3 g, protein 10 g

# APPLE SPICE PUDDING

10 SERVINGS

This rich, fragrant dish has the consistency of a bread pudding. It is best served warm with the cream sauce. (Well, actually, it's also excellent cold with just a little milk or cream poured overtop...)

3 tablespoons butter, softened

3 cups puréed pink or kidney beans

1 teaspoon baking powder

1 teaspoon baking soda

3 eggs

2 teaspoons vanilla

¼ teaspoon ground ginger

½ teaspoon nutmeg

2 teaspoons cinnamon

1 cup brown sugar

½ cup oil

3 medium apples, peeled and cut into slices ¼ inch thick

¾ cup finely chopped walnuts

½ cup raisins (optional)

(There is no flour.)

Preheat oven to 350° F. Grease a 9 x 13-inch baking dish.

Mix butter, puréed beans, baking powder, baking soda, and eggs in a large bowl. Beat well. Add vanilla, ginger, nutmeg, and cinnamon; stir to mix. Add sugar and oil; mix well.

Stir in apples, walnuts, and raisins.

Pour batter into prepared baking dish and bake for 35 to 40 minutes or until a knife inserted in the center of the cake comes out clean.

## Cream Sauce

3 large egg yolks

⅓ cup sugar or Splenda

1 cup light cream

1 tablespoon bourbon (optional)

Whisk together the egg yolks and sugar in a medium bowl until slightly thick.

In a medium saucepan, heat the cream, stirring, over medium heat until small bubbles form.

Whisk the hot cream into the egg yolk mixture. Return to the saucepan and, stirring constantly over low heat, cook until the sauce is slightly thickened. Remove from heat and continue to stir for 2 minutes.

Let cool for 10 minutes and stir in 1 tablespoon of bourbon.

*Per serving:* calories 421, calories from fat 194, total fat 22 g, cholesterol 83 mg, carbohydrates 50 g, fiber 5 g, protein 9 g

# PEANUT BUTTER COOKIES

36 COOKIES

These are the cookies from the junior high school cafeteria for which we handed over the outrageous sum of twenty-five cents each. The taste is the same; only the ingredients are different. Feel free to make them the same giganto size they were back then.

---

1 15.5-ounce can pink beans, drained and rinsed

3 tablespoons water

2½ cups flour

1½ teaspoons baking powder

1 teaspoon baking soda

pinch of salt

¼ cup canola oil

1 cup peanut butter

1½ sticks soft butter (12 tablespoons)

1 cup packed brown sugar

2 eggs

1 tablespoon vanilla

⅓ cup powdered sugar

---

Preheat oven to 350°F. Grease cookie sheet.

In a food processor or blender, purée the beans with 3 tablespoons of water until smooth.

Whisk together the flour, baking powder, baking soda, and salt.

In a large bowl, combine the canola oil, peanut butter, butter, and brown sugar. Beat on medium speed until light and fluffy. Add the eggs and vanilla. Beat once more and stir in the bean purée.

Stir in the powdered sugar and the flour mixture.

Let the dough sit for 5 minutes. Rip off pieces and roll into 1-inch balls (unless you choose to make the huge cookies). Place on a greased cookie sheet 2 inches apart. Press the tines of a fork flat onto each cookie ball, forming a crosshatch pattern.

Bake for 9 to 12 minutes until golden brown. Let cookies set for 1 or 2 minutes before removing from cookie sheet.

*Per cookie:* calories 162, calories from fat 82, total fat 9 g, cholesterol 24 mg, carbohydrates 16 g, fiber 1 g, protein 4 g

# PUMPKIN PECAN CRANBERRY AND BEAN BREAD

24 SLICES

All the flavors and colors of autumn are combined into this sinfully rich bread that is also sinlessly healthy.

---

3 cups flour

1 tablespoon cinnamon

1 teaspoon baking powder

2 teaspoons baking soda

⅔ cup milk

2 teaspoons vanilla

1 15.5-ounce can pink beans, drained and rinsed

2–3 tablespoons water

1 cup canola oil

1½ cups brown sugar (or 1½ cup Splenda or 1 cup maple syrup)

2 eggs

1 15-ounce can pumpkin

6 ounces dried cranberries

¾ cup chopped pecans

---

Preheat oven to 350°F. Grease 3 8-inch loaf pans.

Whisk together the flour, cinnamon, baking powder, and baking soda.

In a small bowl, mix milk and vanilla.

Purée the beans in a food processor or blender with 2 to 3 tablespoons of water until smooth.

In a large mixing bowl, beat the oil and brown sugar until fluffy. Add the eggs and beat again. Stir in the pumpkin and puréed beans. Add the milk and vanilla mixture and beat once more.

Stir in the flour mixture with a rubber spatula, stirring well and scraping the sides of the bowl.

Fold in the dried cranberries and pecans.

Pour batter into three 8-inch greased loaf pans.

Bake for 45 to 50 minutes or until a knife inserted into the center of a loaf comes out clean.

Warm, cold, plain, or with cream cheese and great for breakfast, lunch, or dessert—any possible way or time of day suits this delicious bread.

*Per slice:* calories 309, calories from fat 106, total fat 12 g, cholesterol 1 mg, carbohydrates 47 g, fiber 3 g, protein 4 g

# Lentils

# Lentils

Regular · Red Chief · Pardina · Crimson · Eston

Lentils have been a staple of humankind ever since the Neolithic period, when we changed from hunters and food gatherers to domesticators of wild animals and farmers. Archaeologists have dated remains of wheat, peas, and lentils found at Halicar, an ancient Greek settlement in present-day Turkey, at about 5500 B.C. In ancient Rome, shepherds and senators alike dined on lentils.

This small, lens-shaped cousin of the bean comes in a variety of sizes and colors. Their shape, the lens, is also the Latin word for lentil. Their colors range from brown and brown-green, to red-orange and yellow. Lentils are widely used throughout the Middle East and are very popular in India, where they are cooked down to a purée called dal and used in the famous Indian crackers, pappadams, which are made from lentil flour. Lentil soup seems to be the most popular lentil treat in the United States.

Lentils are one of the few dry beans that don't require soaking. Lentils are never used fresh, but are dried as soon as they are ripe. It is important to thoroughly pick through and wash them to remove any impurities or small stones. You must avoid overcooking lentils, as, unlike other beans, they rapidly turn to mush if cooked too long. Brown lentils will cook in 30 to 40 minutes. The orange and yellow varieties take about 25 minutes.

· · · ·

The U.S. Public Health Service recommends that all women of child-bearing age consume 400 micrograms of folic acid per day. One cup of cooked lentils provides 90 percent of the recommended daily allowance. In fact, lentils provide more folic acid than any other unfortified food. They are also an excellent source of iron. Eating lentils together with foods rich in vitamin C helps the body absorb iron much more efficiently. The only protein that lentils lack is methionine, but consuming them with a grain, eggs, seeds, or dairy product creates the perfect protein.

Here are some of the more common lentil varieties available:

**U.S. REGULAR**—The brown lentil, the most common type in the United States.

**RED CHIEF**—Very quick cooking (as in 5 to 10 minutes). A very beautiful color addition to any dish.

**PARDINA**—Grown mostly in Spain, often called Spanish Brown.

**ESTON**—Used in French cooking, largely produced in Canada.

**CRIMSON**—Another beautifully colored lentil.

### Nutritional values for 1 cup of cooked lentils

Calories 229   Protein 17.8 g   Carbohydrates 39.8 g   Total fat 0.75 g   Fiber 15.6 g
Iron 6.6 mg   Potassium 730 mg   Folate 357 mcg   Niacin 2.1 mg

## APPETIZERS

*Curry Sesame Pâté*

*Lentil Veggie Dip*

*Dal with Red Lentils*

*Lentil Tostadas*

## SALADS, SOUPS & SIDES

*Tomato and Lentil Salad*

*Hot Spinach and Lentil Salad*

*Lentil Salad*

*Sherried Lentil Soup*

*Lemon Lentil Soup*

*Moroccan-style Lentil Soup*

*Red Lentil and Pumpkin Soup*

*Southwest Lentil Pilaf*

*Lentils with Escarole and Lemon*

*Lentil Bread of the Bible*

## MAIN DISHES

*Lentils with Mussels or Clams*

*Pasta e Lenticchie*

*Spinach Fettuccini with Red Lentil
   Sauce*

*Lentil Chili*

*Greek Lentils and Pasta*

*Lentil Burgers*

*Lentil Stew*

*Stuffed Peppers*

*Asian Lentil and Rice Patties*

*Meatless Meatloaf with Cheddar
   Cheese*

*Sweet Potato Lentil Burgers*

## DESSERTS

*Lentil Spice Nut Bread*

*Mocha Lentil Cake*

*Gingerbread*

# Appetizers

## CURRY SESAME PÂTÉ

6 SERVINGS

This baked pâté makes for an elegant presentation and delicious start to any meal.

---

2 tablespoons vegetable oil

1 small onion, finely chopped

1 tablespoon pressed garlic

2 teaspoons curry powder

¼ teaspoon turmeric

½ teaspoon chili powder

½ teaspoon cumin seeds

1 tablespoon tahini (sesame paste)

2½ cups water

1 cup dried lentils, washed and picked through

1 teaspoon kosher salt

2 eggs

¼ cup milk

---

Preheat oven to 400° F.

Heat the vegetable oil in a saucepan; add onion, garlic, curry, turmeric, chili powder, and cumin seeds and sauté until onion is soft.

Stir in tahini. Add water and lentils, bring to a boil, reduce heat, and simmer for 40 to 45 minutes, until lentils are tender.

Transfer lentil mixture to a blender or food processor with salt, eggs, and milk. Purée until smooth. Adjust seasonings, adding more chili if desired. Pour into a buttered terrine or casserole. Cover and bake for 50 to 60 minutes.

This can be served warm or chilled. Either way, surround the plate with the greenery of curly lettuce or parsley and top with carrot curls and thin slices of a tart green apple. Black pepper water crackers go well with this, and the crisp green apple complements and finishes the taste.

*Per serving:* calories 150, calories from fat 56, total fat 6 g, cholesterol 62 mg, carbohydrates 15 g, fiber 8 g, protein 9 g

# LENTIL VEGGIE DIP

6 SERVINGS

A very flavorful dip for your next party. Use it for cut-up raw veggies, pita wedges, chips, even pretzels.

1¼ cups water

1 cup uncooked lentils, washed and picked through

½ teaspoon salt

1 tablespoon olive oil

6 scallions, chopped (both white and green parts)

1 clove garlic, minced

2 tablespoons fresh chopped parsley

⅛ teaspoon cayenne pepper

¼ teaspoon turmeric

¼ cup water, as needed

¼ cup chopped green olives with pimentos

Combine water, lentils, and salt in a saucepan. Bring to a boil and simmer until lentils are tender, 20 to 25 minutes. Drain, reserving stock.

In a medium skillet, heat oil and sauté scallions and garlic until onions are translucent. Add parsley, cayenne pepper, and turmeric. Stir and cook for 1 minute more.

Combine cooked lentils, cooking water, and onion mixture in a food processor, adding the extra water 1 tablespoon at a time as needed to create a spreadable consistency. Stir in the chopped green olives. Refrigerate 2 hours before serving.

*Per serving:* calories 139, calories from fat 27, total fat 3 g, cholesterol 0 mg, carbohydrates 20 g, fiber 10 g, protein 9 g

# DAL WITH RED LENTILS

8 TO 10 SERVINGS

Dal is the spicy staple of Indian cooking. It is served at almost every meal, usually over rice. Our version is just as spicy, yet we're scooping it up with warm pita wedges at a cocktail party.

---

1½ cups raw red lentils, rinsed and picked through

4 cups water

1 medium onion, diced

2 cloves garlic, minced

1 teaspoon grated fresh ginger

1 teaspoon ground cumin

1 teaspoon turmeric

pinch of nutmeg

salt to taste

1–2 small hot green chilies or jalapeño peppers, seeded and minced

1 plum tomato, diced

2 tablespoons fresh cilantro

3–4 large pita rounds

---

Combine the lentils with 3 cups of water in a large saucepan. Add onion, garlic, ginger, cumin, turmeric, and nutmeg. Bring to a boil, reduce heat, cover, and simmer for about 25 to 30 minutes or until lentils are very mushy. Transfer to a food processor or blender and purée until smooth. Return to saucepan and stir in salt. Simmer over low heat until mixture is thickened, about 15 to 20 minutes. Stir in the minced green chilies, tomato, and cilantro.

Cut each pita round into 8 wedges and warm in a hot oven. If you prefer a crunchy pita, spray each wedge with olive oil spray and place on a cookie sheet in a 400° F oven for 8 to 10 minutes or until crisp.

Serve the dip warm in a bowl surrounded by pita wedges and sprigs of fresh cilantro.

*Per serving:* calories 137, calories from fat 7, total fat 1 g, cholesterol 0 mg, carbohydrates 24 g, fiber 4 g, protein 10 g

# LENTIL TOSTADAS

8 TO 10 SERVINGS

A great starter for a Mexican-night dinner or buffet. You can make these as spicy as you wish or leave the red pepper out and put it on the table for individual sprinkling.

---

2 cups water

1 cup lentils, washed and picked through

8 ounces tomato sauce

2 garlic cloves, minced

2 tablespoons chili powder

1 teaspoon cumin

½ teaspoon red pepper flakes

4–5 whole-wheat tortillas

½ cup shredded Monterey Jack cheese

½ cup shredded cheddar cheese

4 cups shredded lettuce

2 tomatoes, chopped

mild or medium salsa

1 cup sour cream

4 scallions, chopped (both white and green parts)

---

Preheat oven to 400° F.

In a medium saucepan, combine water and lentils. Bring to a boil, cover, reduce heat, and simmer for 25 to 30 minutes, stirring occasionally.

Drain and rinse lentils.

In the saucepan, combine tomato sauce, garlic, chili powder, cumin, and red pepper flakes. Add the lentils and simmer over medium heat for 20 minutes, stirring occasionally.

Heat the tortillas on a baking sheet in the preheated oven until crispy, about 5 to 7 minutes.

Cover each tortilla with the warm lentil mixture. Top with both cheeses, lettuce, tomatoes, and salsa. Put a dollop of sour cream over each and sprinkle with the chopped scallions.

Cut each tostada into 4 wedges and serve immediately.

Serve this with a little sangria to wash the spice away if you've overdone it with the red pepper flakes. Some cool slices of avocado come in handy if you've *really* overdone it with the red pepper flakes.

*Per serving:* calories 236, calories from fat 70, total fat 8 g, cholesterol 20 mg, carbohydrates 30 g, fiber 10 g, protein 13 g

# Salads, Soups & Sides

## TOMATO AND LENTIL SALAD

4 SERVINGS

The uses for lentils in salads are limitless. Hopefully these recipes will be but a spur to your imagination to create new and wonderful combinations of your own.

1 quart water

1 teaspoon salt

1 cup dried lentils, rinsed and picked through

1 bay leaf

½ cup minced red onion

¼ cup minced fresh parsley

2 cloves garlic, minced

½ cup canned whole tomatoes, drained and chopped

¼ cup diced celery

¼ cup diced carrots

1 tablespoon balsamic vinegar

½ teaspoon Worcestershire sauce

⅛ teaspoon (or more) Tabasco sauce

fresh ground black pepper to taste

1 teaspoon sugar or sweetener (optional)

3 tablespoons vegetable oil

Bring water and salt to boil in a 2-quart saucepan. Add lentils and the bay leaf. Reduce heat, cover, and simmer for 30 to 40 minutes, until lentils are tender but not mushy. Drain well and discard bay leaf. Transfer lentils to a serving bowl and stir in the onions, parsley, garlic, tomatoes, celery, and carrots.

In a small bowl or jar, combine vinegar, Worcestershire sauce, Tabasco, black pepper, sugar, and oil. Whisk or shake well.

Pour dressing over lentil mixture and toss gently but thoroughly. Cover with plastic wrap and refrigerate for at least 30 minutes.

This is a fine side dish for just about any type of dinner. Serve over some leafy greens to create an extra spot of color on each dish.

*Per serving:* calories 277, calories from fat 98, total fat 11 g, cholesterol 0 mg, carbohydrates 32 g, fiber 16 g, protein 14 g

# HOT SPINACH AND LENTIL SALAD

4 SERVINGS

This earthy combination of mushrooms, spinach, and lentils makes for a perfect side dish on crisp autumn nights.

1 cup lentils, brown or green, washed and picked through

2 teaspoons mustard seed

2 cups vegetable broth

4 slices soy bacon

1 small onion, diced

1 teaspoon garlic, minced

¼ cup water

2 tablespoons sugar

¼ cup cider vinegar

8 cups fresh chopped spinach

2 hard-boiled eggs, chopped

½ cup water chestnuts, chopped

½ red onion, thinly sliced

1 cup thinly sliced white mushrooms

Rinse and drain lentils.

In a large saucepan, over high heat, combine lentils, mustard seed, and broth. Bring to a boil and boil for 1 minute.

Reduce heat to low and simmer for about 25 minutes until lentils are tender, stirring occasionally. Drain lentils.

In a large skillet, cook bacon until crisp. Crumble the bacon. Wipe out skillet and sauté diced onion and garlic in ¼ cup of water for 2 minutes over medium heat.

Add sugar, vinegar, and lentils. Heat for 3 minutes, reducing liquid, stirring constantly.

Add spinach, bacon, hard-boiled eggs, and water chestnuts to lentil mixture and toss until spinach wilts. Top with sliced red onion and sliced mushrooms.

Serve warm, as a side dish

*Per serving: calories 317, calories from fat 46, total fat 5 g, cholesterol 122 mg, carbohydrates 49 g, fiber 18 g, protein 22 g*

# LENTIL SALAD

2 TO 3 SERVINGS

Colorful, fiber-full, and healthful—
need I say more? Do you need
more?

2 cups fresh watercress

1 cup cooked lentils, any color

¼ cup chopped yellow pepper

½ cup chopped green pepper

½ cup chopped red pepper

¼ cup chopped red onion

¼ cup chopped celery

1 cup grape or cherry tomatoes,
sliced in half

Combine above ingredients and lightly
toss with the following dressing.

## Dressing

¼ cup olive oil

2 tablespoons balsamic vinegar

½ teaspoon Dijon mustard

1 splash Worcestershire sauce

¼ teaspoon Splenda (or other no
calorie sweetener)

Whisk together all ingredients and
pour over the salad.

Serve, perhaps, on a large trimmed leaf
of romaine lettuce.

*Per serving:* calories 275, calories from fat
164, total fat 19 g, cholesterol 0 mg, carbohydrates 22 g, fiber 8 g, protein 8 g

# SHERRIED LENTIL SOUP

8 SERVINGS

This splendid soup is distinctive enough to serve at a dinner party as a first course or to spoil your loved ones with on a weeknight. The sherry adds a richness in flavor that disguises the low fat content of this dish.

1 large onion, diced

2 tablespoons olive oil

1 stalk celery, diced

2 small carrots, peeled and diced

1½ cup lentils, rinsed and picked through

4 cups chicken broth (or vegetable broth)

2 cups water

1 large potato, peeled and diced

salt and freshly ground black pepper to taste

2 tablespoons unsalted butter

1 tablespoon minced garlic

1 teaspoon ground cumin

1 teaspoon dried parsley

medium dry sherry

Set aside 2 tablespoons of the diced onion.

Heat oil in a soup pot. Add onions, celery, and carrots, cooking over medium heat until onions are soft. Add lentils, broth, and water. Bring to a boil, reduce heat, cover, and simmer for 25 minutes. Add the diced potato and cook for another 30 minutes until lentils are very soft.

Strain the soup through a colander into a large bowl, saving the liquid. Return the liquid to the soup pot; transfer the lentils and vegetables into a food processor and purée until smooth. Add this to the liquid in the pot. Season with salt and pepper. Bring soup to a gentle simmer.

In a small skillet, melt butter and add garlic and reserved onion. Sauté until just softened. Stir in cumin and parsley.

Add mixture to the soup.

Warm those soup bowls and serve this soup with a splash of sherry over each serving.

If you aren't just charming guests with a delicious first course, a watercress and cucumber salad would make this a perfect midweek meal.

*Per serving:* calories 226, calories from fat 65, total fat 7 g, cholesterol 18 mg, carbohydrates 28 g, fiber 12 g, protein 13 g

## LEMON LENTIL SOUP

4 SERVINGS

This creamy, lemony soup is light and soothing. Virtually fat free with 25 grams of protein, this soup has it all.

4 cups chicken broth (or water)

3 medium carrots, chopped

1 large onion, chopped

2 stalks celery, chopped

1½ cups red chief lentils, washed and picked through

1 teaspoon minced garlic

juice of 1 fresh lemon

salt and pepper to taste

up to 1 cup water

1 cup cooked white rice

4 lemon slices

¼ cup chopped fresh parsley

In a saucepan, combine the chicken broth or water, carrots, onion, and celery. Bring to a boil and simmer until the onions are clear. Add the lentils, garlic, lemon juice, salt and pepper. Continue to simmer for 5 to 10 more minutes or until the lentils are soft.

Transfer the soup into a blender or food processor and blend until creamy smooth, adding up to one cup of water to thin if it is too thick. Return mixture to the saucepan, add the cooked rice, and reheat until warmed through.

Serve this delightful soup garnished with a lemon slice and chopped parsley.

*Per serving:* calories 381, calories from fat 28, total fat 3 g, cholesterol 0 mg, carbohydrates 65 g, fiber 11 g, protein 25 g

# MOROCCAN-STYLE LENTIL SOUP

12 SERVINGS

This wonderfully exotic blend of flavors and vegetables is from the kitchen of Lauren Blair, one of my oldest and dearest friends. This creation is a perfect reflection of Lauren's artistic abilities, on canvas as well as in the kitchen.

---

2 tablespoons butter

2 tablespoons olive oil

2 medium onions, finely chopped

1 small green bell pepper, finely chopped

3 carrots, peeled and shredded

1 cup finely chopped zucchini

2 cups peeled and finely chopped eggplant

2 tablespoons minced garlic

2 teaspoons cumin

1 teaspoon curry powder

¾ teaspoon allspice

1½ teaspoons cinnamon

red pepper flakes to taste

2 quarts water

2 14.5-ounce cans chicken broth (or vegetable broth)

1 cup dry sherry

1 14-ounce can diced tomatoes, drained

1 16-ounce bag dried lentils, washed and picked through

salt and pepper to taste

yogurt or sour cream to garnish

1 bunch fresh cilantro, chopped

---

In a large soup pot, combine butter and oil and stir until butter has melted. Add the onions, green pepper, carrots, zucchini, eggplant, and garlic. Stir well. Stir in the cumin, curry powder, allspice, cinnamon, and red pepper flakes. Sauté until vegetables have softened, about 10 minutes. Add water, chicken or vegetable broth, sherry, tomatoes, and lentils and bring to a boil. Reduce heat to low and simmer, uncovered, for 40 to 50 minutes or until lentils have softened. Season with salt and pepper.

Garnish each serving with a dollop of yogurt or sour cream and a sprinkling of chopped cilantro.

Have a basket of warm Moroccan bread on hand. A fresh tomato and cucumber salad goes beautifully with this.

*Per serving:* calories 236, calories from fat 46, total fat 5 g, cholesterol 5 mg, carbohydrates 31 g, fiber 14 g, protein 13 g

# RED LENTIL AND PUMPKIN SOUP

8 SERVINGS

This soup is just the most *beautiful* pumpkin color. It's perfect for an autumn table. Be a little daring and serve this as a totally different starter for Thanksgiving dinner.

1 large onion, chopped

1 cup chopped celery

2 tablespoons olive oil

2 teaspoons minced garlic

4½ cups chicken broth (or vegetable broth)

1 pound red lentils, washed and picked through

1 15-ounce can pumpkin (not pumpkin pie mix)

sea salt and freshly ground black pepper to taste

fresh flat-leaf parsley sprigs

In a food processor, process the onion and celery until puréed.

In a large soup pot, heat olive oil and add the puréed onion and celery. Stir in the garlic and sauté until the purée is translucent.

Add the broth and lentils. Bring to a boil. Reduce heat and simmer gently for 20 to 25 minutes or until lentils are tender. Stir occasionally. Add the canned pumpkin and stir to mix well. Simmer for only up to 5 minutes or until pumpkin is heated. (If you simmer the mixture longer, the soup will acquire a pulpy consistency.) If the soup is a bit too thick, add some water to thin it out.

Season with salt and pepper.

Garnish with a sprig of the parsley.

I cannot tell you how beautiful this will look in a big white soup tureen, if you have one.

*Per serving:* calories 243, calories from fat 47, total fat 5 g, cholesterol 0 mg, carbohydrates 35 g, fiber 7 g, protein 16 g

# SOUTHWEST LENTIL PILAF

6 SERVINGS

This recipe uses brilliant-colored red chief lentils, which lend to the beauty of this dish. Quick, extremely nutritious, and very pleasing to the eye.

---

2 cups chicken broth (or vegetable broth)

¾ cup water

⅔ cup quick-cooking rice

½ cup red chief lentils, washed and picked through

1 can white beans, drained and rinsed

½ red onion, finely chopped

¼ cup chopped red bell pepper

¼ cup chopped green bell pepper

1 cup mild salsa

1 cup corn kernels

½ teaspoon chili powder

1 teaspoon minced garlic

8 fresh tomato slices

¼ cup chopped fresh cilantro

---

Heat the broth and water to boiling. Add the rice and lentils and cook for 5 to 7 minutes. Add the remaining ingredients except the tomato slices and cilantro and bring back to a boil. Reduce heat and simmer for 10 minutes.

Top each serving with 2 tomato slices and chopped cilantro.

*Per serving:* calories 418, calories from fat 18, total fat 2 g, cholesterol 0 mg, carbohydrates 78 g, fiber 14 g, protein 25 g

# LENTILS WITH ESCAROLE AND LEMON

6 SERVINGS

This is a variation on an Arabic dish that is very soup-like, yet traditionally is served as a side dish. The blend of garlic and lemon flavors makes this exceptionally nutritious dish uniquely tasteful.

4 cups water

1½ cups dried lentils, washed and picked through

1 large head escarole, well washed and chopped

¼ cup extra virgin olive oil

1 cup chopped onions

5 garlic cloves, crushed

1 teaspoon kosher salt

1 bunch cilantro, chopped

juice of 1 lemon

1–2 teaspoons flour

sesame oil for seasoning

In a saucepan, combine water and lentils, bring to a boil, reduce heat, and simmer for 30 minutes or until tender. Add the chopped escarole to the lentils and continue to cook until the escarole is soft.

In a skillet, heat olive oil and add chopped onions. Sauté until the onions are light brown. Add the crushed garlic cloves along with the salt to the olive oil and onions. Stir until garlic starts to brown, then stir in the cilantro. Transfer the olive oil mixture to the saucepan with the lentils and escarole.

Mix the lemon juice with 1 to 2 teaspoons of flour and add to the saucepan to thicken the sauce. Simmer until it is like a thick soup.

Serve hot, with the sesame oil available for individual drizzling overtop.

*Per serving:* calories 281, calories from fat 87, total fat 10 g, cholesterol 0 mg, carbohydrates 35 g, fiber 18 g, protein 16 g

# LENTIL BREAD OF THE BIBLE

4 LOAVES, 24 SLICES

This is the 2002 version of Ezekiel's bread of the Bible (Ezekiel 4:9):

"TAKE THOU ALSO UNTO THEE WHEAT, AND BARLEY, AND BEANS AND LENTILS, AND MILLET, AND FITCHES,* AND PUT THEM INTO ONE VESSEL, AND MAKE THEE BREAD THEREOF..."

As it was in the beginning, is now, and ever shall be, this heavenly bread is jam-packed with protein, calcium, phosphorus, iron, sodium, potassium, vitamins A and C, thiamine, riboflavin, and niacin. It seems almost too much health to put in one mouthful.

8 cups wheat flour

4 cups barley flour

2 cups soy flour

½ cup millet flour

¼ cup rye flour

4 packets yeast

1 cup warm water (about 100–110°F)

½ to ¾ cup honey

1 cup lentils, cooked and mashed

4–5 tablespoons olive oil

4 cups water

1 tablespoon salt

Combine flours in bowl and set aside.

Dissolve yeast in 1 cup warm water and 1 tablespoon of the honey. Set aside 10 minutes.

Blend lentils, oil, remaining honey, and a small amount of water in a blender (or a rock bowl with a stone for mixing as they would have back then...). Place in a large mixing bowl with remaining water. Stir in two cups of flour mixture. Add the yeast mixture. Stir in salt and remaining flour.

Place on floured board and knead until smooth. Put dough in an oiled bowl. Let rise until double in bulk, about 1 hour. Punch down and knead again. Cut dough into four portions and shape into four large loaves. Place in greased loaf pans and let rise until double in bulk, again, about 1 hour.

Bake at 375°F for 45 minutes to 1 hour.

Eat and heal.

*The "fitches" called for in the Bible seem to refer to some seasoning herb. Some suggestions might be cumin, fennel, or nutmeg. They are optional in this recipe, so use your imagination and create your own taste.

*Per slice:* calories 358, calories from fat 39, total fat 5 g, cholesterol 0 mg, carbohydrates 68 g, fiber 5 g, protein 13 g

# Main Dishes

## LENTILS WITH MUSSELS OR CLAMS

In ancient Rome, shepherds and senators alike consumed lentils. Apicius, a Roman who lived in the first century, included several recipes for lentils in a cookbook, one of the world's oldest, entitled *De Re Coquinaria*. The following recipe is a literal translation of the original Latin recipe, *Lenticula*. It seems that Apicius wrote for what would be considered experienced chefs, since he seldom specified quantities or procedure details.

If you're feeling brave, give this a try!

Put lentils to soak in a kettle with ample water; after several hours bring to a boil and reduce heat to simmer.

Combine freshly ground black pepper with ground cumin and coriander seeds, a minced mint leaf, and a pinch of fresh thyme; moisten with vinegar. Add honey, soy sauce, and wine or grape juice which has been condensed by boiling, then add to lentils.

When lentils are done, mince and add boiled mussels or minced clams. Cook and stir lentils until liquid is reduced or thicken with a paste of flour and water. Transfer to a heated dish and pour a little olive oil over the lentil-mussel mixture.

Hmmmm...

# PASTA E LENTICCHIE (Pasta and Lentils)

8 SERVINGS

A twist on the standard Italian pasta fagiole.

2 carrots

2 ribs celery

1 large onion

6 cups water

1 16-ounce bag lentils, rinsed and picked through

1 teaspoon salt

1 pound spaghetti

¼ cup olive oil

2 cloves garlic, sliced

¼ cup chopped fresh parsley

Dice carrots, celery, and onion. Place in a pot with water and the rinsed lentils. Bring to a slow boil and leave to simmer for 40 to 50 minutes, stirring regularly. Turn off the heat and add salt to the water; cover and let sit for 5 minutes. Drain.

Prepare spaghetti according to package directions for al dente. Drain spaghetti and return to the pot.

In a skillet, heat olive oil and brown garlic lightly.

Top the spaghetti with the lentil mixture and the olive oil with the garlic. Toss to mix. Add parsley and toss again.

Drizzle with extra olive oil and salt to taste.

This protein-laden dish needs a green salad to set off the green of the parsley and to round out the meal.

*Per serving:* calories 414, calories from fat 71, total fat 8 g, cholesterol 0 mg, carbohydrates 67 g, fiber 17 g, protein 20 g

# SPINACH FETTUCCINI WITH RED LENTIL SAUCE

6 SERVINGS

It takes minutes, just minutes, to prepare this outrageously delicious and colorful meal. Two of the key factors here are the fresh Parmesan and the wine you choose to accompany dinner.

---

¾ pound spinach fettuccini mix [half regular (semolina) pasta and half spinach pasta]

1 tablespoon olive oil

2 tablespoons butter

2 tablespoons extra virgin olive oil

1 tablespoon minced garlic

1 large onion, minced

1 cup red lentils, washed and picked through

3 tablespoons tomato paste

1 tablespoon chopped fresh parsley

1 tablespoon chopped fresh basil

2¼ cups boiling water

kosher salt and freshly ground black pepper to taste

coarsely grated fresh Parmesan cheese to taste

---

Follow the directions on the fettuccini box for *al dente*, adding 1 tablespoon of olive oil to the boiling water. Drain and return to the saucepan. Add 2 tablespoons butter and stir. Cover and set aside to keep warm.

In another large saucepan, heat 2 tablespoons extra virgin olive oil and sauté the garlic and onion for about 5 minutes, stirring occasionally. Add the lentils, tomato paste, parsley, basil, and boiling water. Return to a boil, reduce heat, and simmer for 20 minutes, stirring occasionally until lentils are soft.

Season with salt and pepper.

Reheat the fettuccini gently if necessary.

Top with the lentil sauce; garnish with sprigs of fresh basil.

Serve with tons of the freshly grated Parmesan cheese.

Relax and enjoy this extremely simple meal with a full-bodied Chianti. Delicious!

*Per serving:* calories 428, calories from fat 108, total fat 12 g, cholesterol 10 mg, carbohydrates 64 g, fiber 5 g, protein 16 g

# LENTIL CHILI

6 SERVINGS

Chili needs cornbread and this one is no exception. Make a nice buttermilk cornbread and serve it hot with this delicious version of an all-time favorite.

---

3 tablespoons oil

1 medium onion, chopped

1 green bell pepper, chopped

2 cloves garlic, minced

2 14.5-ounce cans chicken broth (or vegetable broth)

1½ cans water

1½ cups lentils, rinsed and picked through

2 teaspoons cumin powder

1 tablespoon chili powder

¼ cup tomato paste

¼ cup ketchup

1 tablespoon apple cider vinegar

---

In a large saucepan or soup pot, heat oil and add onion and bell pepper. Sauté, stirring until the onions are translucent. Add garlic, broth, and water.

Stir in rinsed lentils. Add cumin, chili powder, tomato paste, and ketchup. Bring to a boil, reduce heat, and simmer uncovered for up to 1 hour, or until lentils are soft. Add more liquid as needed.

*Just before serving*, stir in the vinegar.

A little shredded cheddar with a dollop of sour cream and some chopped scallions would do this no harm.

*Per serving:* calories 282, calories from fat 75, total fat 8 g, cholesterol 1 mg, carbohydrates 36 g, fiber 16 g, protein 18 g

# GREEK LENTILS AND PASTA

4 SERVINGS

This versatile dish can be served warm during the winter or cold in summertime. The flavors of the lemon, mint, and feta combine to create a classic Greek taste.

---

½ cup lentils, washed and picked through

2 cups chicken broth (or vegetable broth or water)

8 ounces rotini pasta

3 tablespoons extra virgin olive oil (divided use)

3 cloves garlic, minced

1 cup chopped onion

½ pound fresh green beans, cut into 1-inch pieces

2 cups grape tomatoes, halved

juice of ½ lemon

2 tablespoons capers, drained

½ cup fresh parsley, chopped

⅓ cup fresh mint, chopped

1 teaspoon dried basil (or 2 teaspoons fresh, chopped)

½ teaspoon salt

freshly ground black pepper to taste

4 ounces feta cheese, crumbled

---

Bring lentils and broth to boil in a medium-size saucepan. Reduce heat, cover, and simmer 30 to 40 minutes or until lentils are tender, but not mushy. Drain and set aside in a colander. Cook pasta according to package directions for *al dente*. Drain over the lentils in the colander.

While the pasta and lentils are cooking, heat the oil in a large skillet over medium heat. Add the garlic and onion and sauté, stirring, for 2 minutes. Add the green beans and cook for another 5 to 6 minutes, stirring occasionally, until they are just tender.

Stir in tomatoes, lemon juice, capers, parsley, mint, basil, salt, and pepper. Remove from heat.

Toss the lentils, pasta, and vegetable mixture together.

Stir in the feta cheese.

A spinach salad and a hearty red wine is what I would serve with this meal of colors!

*Per serving:* calories 536, calories from fat 163, total fat 18 g, cholesterol 25 mg, carbohydrates 72 g, fiber 13 g, protein 23 g

# LENTIL BURGERS

10 BURGERS

The deep, nutty flavor of the lentils, combined with the crunch and extra nutrition of the sunflower seeds, contributes to the excellence of this healthy lunch.

---

4 cups water

½ cup brown lentils, washed and picked through

½ cup barley

½ cup brown rice

3 tablespoons olive oil

1½ cups shredded carrots

1 medium onion, minced

2 stalks celery, minced

¼ cup toasted or dry roasted sunflower seeds

1 teaspoon salt

freshly ground black pepper to taste

1 teaspoon minced thyme

2 tablespoons minced fresh basil

2 tablespoons fresh chopped parsley

2 teaspoons minced garlic

2 large eggs

½ cup flour

3 tablespoons vegetable oil

---

In a large saucepan, bring the water to a boil, add lentils, reduce heat, cover, and simmer for 15 minutes. Add the barley; cover and simmer for 15 more minutes. Add brown rice; cover tightly and simmer for 20 minutes or until water is absorbed. If you need to add more water, stir in a small amount so that the pan does not go dry.

Remove from heat and set aside.

Heat the olive oil in a medium skillet and add carrots, onion, and celery. Sauté until the vegetables are tender, about 10 minutes. Add sunflower seeds, salt, pepper, thyme, basil, parsley, and garlic. Stir for 1 to 2 more minutes. Remove from heat. Combine grains and vegetables in a large covered container and refrigerate overnight.

When you are ready to cook, add the eggs and flour to the refrigerated grain mixture. Mix well. For each burger, form the mixture into a 4-inch ball and flatten to about ¾-inch thick.

In a large skillet, heat the vegetable oil over medium heat. Add the burgers and cook until golden brown on both sides, about 3 to 4 minutes.

Serve on warm whole-wheat buns with fat slices of fresh tomato and red onion.

*Per burger:* calories 248, calories from fat 105, total fat 12 g, cholesterol 49 mg, carbohydrates 30 g, fiber 6 g, protein 7 g

# LENTIL STEW

4 SERVINGS

All you need for this dinner is a cold winter night. A fireplace would be nice, but a cozy couch and a blanket will do.

---

¼ cup olive oil

2 medium onions, sliced

2 pounds potatoes, unpeeled, washed, and cut into 1-inch chunks

1 pound carrots, sliced into ½-inch sections

4 stalks celery, sliced

½ pound mushrooms, sliced

½ cup dried brown lentils, washed and picked through

2 tablespoons flour

2 teaspoons thyme

5 cups water

¼ cup soy sauce

kosher or sea salt and ground black pepper to taste

chopped parsley

---

Heat oil in a large saucepan over medium heat and sauté the onion until soft but not brown, about 3 to 4 minutes.

Add the potatoes, carrots, celery, mushrooms, and lentils and stir to mix. Sprinkle in the flour and thyme and stir once more.

Add the water, soy sauce, salt, and pepper. Bring to a boil and stir again. Reduce heat, cover, and simmer until the lentils are tender, about 40 to 50 minutes, stirring occasionally.

Top each serving with the chopped parsley, make a big green leafy salad, and cut a nice crusty bread into good-sized dipping chunks. Then warm yourself to the soul with this hearty dinner.

*Per serving:* calories 519, calories from fat 126, total fat 14 g, cholesterol 0 mg, carbohydrates 87 g, fiber 17 g, protein 17 g

# STUFFED PEPPERS

8 SERVINGS

"Filling" would be a good word. "Delicious," another. But definitely "nutritious." Even a lover of the stuffed peppers of old, such as my husband, found no fault with these.

---

3 tablespoons olive oil

2 medium onions, chopped

1 cup chopped celery

1 tablespoon minced garlic

¼ cup chopped fresh parsley

1 tablespoon dry basil (or 2 tablespoons chopped fresh basil)

1 cup green olives with pimentos, halved

1 6-ounce jar tomato sauce

kosher salt and freshly ground black pepper to taste

1 cup cooked brown basmati rice

3 cups cooked lentils (8 ounces dry)

8 medium green bell peppers, tops cut off and seeded

3 cups tomato sauce, homemade or your favorite brand

1½ cups grated cheddar cheese

In a large skillet, heat olive oil and sauté onions, celery, and garlic until onions are soft. Stir in parsley, basil, and green olives. Sauté for 2 to 3 more minutes. Stir in the jar of tomato sauce and season with salt and pepper. Cook until heated through, 2 to 3 more minutes

In a large bowl, combine the cooked basmati rice, the cooked lentils, and sauce mixture from the skillet.

In a lasagna pan or baking dish, pour 2 cups of sauce into the bottom. Arrange the green bell peppers over the sauce. Stuff each pepper to the top with the lentil filling. Top each pepper with a dollop of tomato sauce. Sprinkle each with grated cheddar cheese. Cover with aluminum foil and bake for 1 hour.

This dish freezes wonderfully. As it is a meal unto itself, having this ready to pop into an oven is a great rescue for a busy day.

*Per serving:* calories 410, calories from fat 140, total fat 16 g, cholesterol 26 mg, carbohydrates 53 g, fiber 12 g, protein 18 g

# ASIAN LENTIL AND RICE PATTIES

4 SERVINGS

These very different patties make a great lunch or dinner.

---

½ cup uncooked brown rice

¼ cup dried brown lentils, washed and picked through

1½ cups water

¼ cup finely chopped cashews

½ teaspoon finely minced garlic

4 scallions, finely chopped (both white and green parts)

1 egg, beaten

2 tablespoons apricot preserves

2 teaspoons soy sauce

ginger vegetable sauce (recipe follows)

2 scallions, chopped for garnish

hot cooked Chinese noodles (rice flour noodles or buckwheat noodles)

---

Heat rice, lentils, and water to boiling in a medium saucepan. Reduce heat to low, cover, and simmer 30 to 40 minutes, stirring occasionally, until lentils are tender and water is absorbed. Cool slightly.

Mash the rice and lentil mixture slightly with a fork. Stir in cashews, garlic, chopped scallions, egg, apricot preserves, and soy sauce. Mix well and shape the mixture into 4 patties, each about ½-inch thick.

Spray a 10-inch nonstick skillet with cooking oil spray. Cook the patties over medium heat about 5 minutes per side, turning once.

Remove patties from pan; keep warm.

## Vegetable Sauce

---

½ cup sliced celery

½ cup sliced carrots

½ teaspoon minced garlic

1 tablespoon slivered fresh ginger

½ cup water

1½ tablespoons apricot preserves

2 teaspoons soy sauce

1 teaspoon cornstarch

---

Heat all ingredients to boiling in the same skillet the patties were cooked in; reduce heat to medium. Simmer for about 5 minutes, stirring occasionally, until the celery and carrots are tender. Add the patties. Cover and cook for 5 more minutes. Serve patties and sauce over the Chinese noodles and garnish with the extra chopped scallions.

*Per serving:* calories 430, calories from fat 52, total fat 7 g, cholesterol 62 mg, carbohydrates 88 g, fiber 6 g, protein 8 g

# MEATLESS MEATLOAF WITH CHEDDAR CHEESE

4 SERVINGS

Move over Wednesday night meatloaf! Here is a much healthier version that's still high in protein.

---

½ pound cheddar cheese, grated

2 cups cooked lentils

1 small onion, chopped

½ teaspoon salt

freshly ground black pepper to taste

¼ teaspoon thyme

1 cup soft bread crumbs, packed

1 egg slightly beaten

1 tablespoon butter, softened

---

Preheat oven to 350° F.

Combine the cheese, lentils, and onion. Add salt, pepper, and thyme. Mix in the bread crumbs, egg, and butter. Make sure mixture is well blended. Bake in a greased loaf pan for 45 minutes.

Serve as you would a meatloaf, with mashed potatoes or a little ketchup on the side, or maybe a bit of tomato sauce.

*Per serving:* calories 388, calories from fat 137, total fat 16 g, cholesterol 99 mg, carbohydrates 41 g, fiber 9 g, protein 21 g

# SWEET POTATO LENTIL BURGERS

4 LARGE BURGERS

Let's see...we have fiber here, protein (lots), beta carotene, and vitamin C, just to mention a few. Not a bad profile for something that tastes absolutely wonderful to boot.

---

2 cups mashed yams or sweet potatoes (about 2 large or 3 medium)

1 tablespoon olive oil

1 medium white onion, diced

1 teaspoon minced garlic

2 cups cooked lentils

½ cup chopped pecans

salt and pepper to taste

1 large tomato, chopped

1 red onion, chopped or thinly sliced

1½ cups shredded lettuce

2 large pita rounds

Mustard-yogurt dressing (recipe follows)

---

Preheat oven to 400° F.

To make the mashed yams, peel and cube the yams or sweet potatoes and boil or steam until done. Blend in a blender or food processor with a little of the cooking liquid until smooth and fluffy.

In a medium skillet, heat the olive oil and sauté the onion and garlic just until the onion is soft. Transfer mixture to a large bowl. Add the lentils, pecans, salt, and pepper and mix well. Form into 4 burgers and place on an oil-sprayed nonstick cookie sheet. Cover with foil and bake for 20 to 25 minutes.

Serve each in a warmed pita half. Top with chopped tomato, red onion slices, shredded lettuce, and the mustard-yogurt dressing.

## Mustard-Yogurt Dressing

---

1 cup low-fat yogurt or sour cream

2 tablespoons prepared spicy mustard

½ teaspoon dill

---

Stir together until completely blended.

*Per serving (without dressing):* calories 433, calories from fat 132, total fat 16 g, cholesterol 0 mg, carbohydrates 63 g, fiber 16 g, protein 15 g

# Desserts

. . . . . . . . . . . . . . . . . . . . . . . . . . . . . .

## LENTIL SPICE NUT BREAD

2 LOAVES, 16 SLICES

Nothing—I repeat, nothing—warms up a home on a chilly day more than the aroma of a baking spice cake. And nothing comforts the senses more than eating that spice cake warm from the oven and knowing that it's almost as nutritious as it is delicious.

1 cup lentils, washed and picked through

2½ cups water

⅔ cup buttermilk

⅔ cup shortening

2 cups brown sugar

4 eggs

3⅓ cups sifted flour

2 teaspoons baking soda

½ teaspoon salt

1 teaspoon baking powder

1 teaspoon cinnamon

½ teaspoon nutmeg

½ teaspoon ground cloves

1 cup chopped walnuts or pecans

Preheat oven to 350° F. Grease two 9 x 5-inch loaf pans.

Combine lentils and water in a medium saucepan and bring to a boil. Simmer for 35 to 40 minutes or until lentils are soft. Drain the lentils. Transfer the lentils to a food processor or blender, add buttermilk, and purée until smooth.

In a large mixing bowl, cream the shortening and brown sugar together. Add the eggs, one at a time, beating between additions. Mix in the lentil and buttermilk mixture.

In a separate bowl, sift together the dry ingredients and stir into the creamed mixture, along with the nuts.

Divide the batter between the 2 prepared loaf pans and bake for 60 to 70 minutes or until a knife inserted in the center of the loaves comes out clean. Cool on a wire rack or dive in and eat warm with cream cheese.

*Per slice:* calories 389, calories from fat 133, total fat 15 g, cholesterol 62 mg, carbohydrates 55 g, fiber 5 g, protein 9 g

## MOCHA LENTIL CAKE

24 PIECES

Protein, fiber, and folic acid in a good old-fashioned chocolate cake; this just doesn't seem likely, but here they are in a very tasty and rich morsel that's not that old-fashioned.

---

2 cups water

⅔ cup lentils, washed and picked through

¼ cup brewed coffee

1½ cup sugar or Splenda

¾ cup cocoa

1 cup cooking oil

4 large eggs

2 teaspoons vanilla

1½ cups sifted flour

1½ teaspoon baking soda

1½ teaspoon baking powder

¼ teaspoon salt

---

Preheat oven to 350° F. Grease and flour a 9 x 12-inch baking pan.

In a saucepan, combine 2 cups of water and the lentils and bring to a boil. Simmer for 40 minutes and then drain lentils.

Place cooked lentils into a food processor or blender with ¼ cup of brewed coffee and purée until smooth.

In a large mixing bowl, combine sugar or Splenda, cocoa, oil, and eggs and beat well for 2 minutes.

Add vanilla and the puréed lentils and mix to blend well.

Stir in flour, baking soda, baking powder, and salt.

Pour batter into prepared pan and bake for 20 to 25 minutes, until a knife inserted in the center comes out clean.

Feel free to sprinkle with a little powdered sugar or slice some strawberries on the side of each serving and top with a little dollop of whipped cream. Above all, don't feel guilty about indulging in this treat.

*Per piece:* calories 149, calories from fat 93, total fat 11 g, cholesterol 41 mg, carbohydrates 11 g, fiber 3 g, protein 4 g

# GINGERBREAD

ABOUT 24 PIECES

Nothing can compare to the smell of gingerbread cooking on a winter afternoon, except maybe eating the gingerbread warm with a little whipped cream. Gingerbread is one of my earliest dessert memories, and this comforting version stands right up to it.

---

1 cup dried brown lentils, washed and picked through

3½ cups water

1 tablespoon butter

½ teaspoon salt

¾ cup vegetable oil

½ cup brown sugar

1 cup molasses

3 large eggs

⅓ cup half-and-half

1½ cups flour

¼ teaspoon salt

½ teaspoon cloves

1 tablespoon ground ginger

2 teaspoons cinnamon

1 teaspoon baking powder

1 teaspoon baking soda

---

Preheat oven to 350° F. Grease and flour a 9 x 13-inch baking dish.

Place the lentils, water, salt, and butter in a saucepan. Cover and bring to a boil. Reduce heat and simmer for 35 to 40 minutes, stirring occasionally. Drain and place the mixture in a food processor or blender. Process until the lentils are smooth.

In a large mixing bowl, cream the oil and brown sugar. Add molasses, beating well. Add eggs and half-and-half, beating again. Combine the purée and sugar mixture and beat on medium speed for 1 minute. Add the rest of the dry ingredients and beat another 3 minutes.

Transfer batter to the prepared cake pan and bake for 35 minutes or until a knife inserted in the center comes out clean.

Absolutely enjoy—and don't forget the whipped cream!

*Per piece:* calories 184, calories from fat 72, total fat 8 g, cholesterol 32 mg, carbohydrates 24 g, fiber 3 g, protein 4 g

# Index